BOOKS IN THE SPECIAL EDUCATION SERIES

READING IS FOR EVERYONE

A Guide for Parents and Teachers of Exceptional Children

DOROTHY JEFFREE
MARGARET SKEFFINGTON

with additional material by
Sally B. Carter, Ed.D., University of Georgia

A SPECTRUM BOOK

Prentice-Hall, Inc.
Englewood Cliffs, New Jersey 07632

Library of Congress Cataloging in Publication Data

Jeffree, Dorothy M.
  Reading is for everyone.

  (Special education series)
  Rev. ed. of: Let me read. c1980.
  "A Spectrum Book."
  Bibliography: p.
  Includes index.
  1. Handicapped children—Education—Reading.
2. Mentally handicapped children—Education—Reading.
3. Reading disability.   4. Reading (Preschool)   5. Reading
readiness.   I. Skeffington, Margaret.   II. Jeffree,
Dorothy M.   Let me read.   III. Title.
LC4028.5.J44   1984   371.9'044   84-8381
ISBN 0-13-755224-6
ISBN 0-13-755216-5 (pbk.)

10 9 8 7 6 5 4 3 2 1

ISBN 0-13-755224-6

ISBN 0-13-755216-5 {PBK.}

Editorial/production supervision by Elizabeth Torjussen
Cover design by Hal Siegel
Manufacturing buyer: Edward J. Ellis

Prentice-Hall International, Inc., *London*
Prentice-Hall of Australia Pty. Limited, *Sydney*
Prentice-Hall Canada Inc., *Toronto*
Prentice-Hall of India Private Limited, *New Delhi*
Prentice-Hall of Japan, Inc., *Tokyo*
Prentice-Hall of Southeast Asia Pte. Ltd., *Singapore*
Whitehall Books Limited, *Wellington, New Zealand*
Editora Prentice-Hall do Brasil Ltda., *Rio de Janeiro*

Contents

Acknowledgments

Many of the ideas and games in this book were developed in the context of the PATH Project which was financed by The Department of Health and Social Security. The project is based at the Hester Adrian Research Centre, University of Manchester, England.

We would like to thank all those who took part in recent experiments in the teaching of reading and prereading to pupils in special schools.

We acknowledge particularly the help of the following:

Mr. I. Selkirk, Headteacher, and his staff, Cromwell Special School, N. Reddish,

Mrs. J. Drugan, Headteacher, and her staff, The Birches, Rusholme, Manchester,

for welcoming us into their schools;

the experienced teachers on the 1978-79 DEHC course (Diploma in the Education of Handicapped Children) in the University of Manchester

for their enthusiasm and ideas in initiating the reading experiments;

and especially:

Mike Marra, Edna Hallam, Nick Hughes, Barbara Stollery, Mike Donough, Eileen Jeffs, Daphne Elrington, Rich McKenzie, Paula Halliday, Gabbi Leah, and Peter Bunting; the 1970-80 group for their continuing help in an extension of the experiment;

Mr. Tony Lonton, Tutor in Charge of DEHC for his co-operation;

Dr. S. Cheseldine of Hester Adrian Research Centre in the University of Manchester for her participation in the experiment;

Miss J. Warner for her helpful suggestions;

Barbara Pendlebury for her dramatic use of a Red Indian story;

the parents of the pupils who played games at home;

Joanna McCulloch for typing the manuscript.

Finally, special thanks go to those pupils who worked with us in the special schools, not just for their cooperation, but for the ideas they contributed themselves.

The authors would like to acknowledge the permission of George Allen & Unwin to publish an extract from *The Hobbit* by J.R.R. Tolkien; and Ginn & Company for permission to publish an extract from *The Pancake* by James H. Fassett, Beacon Books.

Preface

We consider that the ideas and methods described in this book have a general application. They will not be limited in their usefulness to the particular group for whom we are writing: those handicapped pupils and young people that the Warnock report in 1978 proposed should be described as having "severe learning difficulties."

Many of the ideas and methods for building up prereading skills at home could be used by parents of preschool children. They would give their children a good start for school, not by teaching them to read but by stimulating them to enjoy books, to expect pleasure from learning and meaning from print: all good preliminaries for teachers to build on when the children come to school.

Moreover, the book will be useful for those children whose main (if not only) difficulty is learning to read. Some of these are helped by remedial reading, but some show great resistance to it and need very special methods.

It should also help those pupils with moderate learning difficulties—whether in a special school or class—to achieve a higher level of literacy or to set out on the path to literacy.

The teaching of reading and prereading advocated here is meant to have more the flavor of "fun" than of "lessons," yet it belongs to a carefully thought-out system with appropriate aims and goals. In working these out, we have drawn on our own considerable experience of teaching reading, on our research into handicap—particularly that of one of us (Dorothy Jeffree)—and on our experience of teaching handicapped children, as well as on our recent experiments in teaching reading to handicapped children and young people.

The book has been written so that it can be used by both parents and teachers, and we have taken pains to provide guidelines on how these two partners in the education of children can work together or complement each other.

READING
IS FOR
EVERYONE

Introduction

HOW TO USE THIS BOOK

In this introduction, we outline the ideas that underlie the methods we are describing: ideas about the teaching of reading, ideas about the weaknesses and strengths of handicapped children as learners, and ideas about ways of ensuring that learning takes place. Since some people are not convinced that mentally handicapped pupils should learn to read, we have written a short section on this topic. Thus the standpoint from which the book is written can be understood from the start.

But our ideas will also be found again, illustrated in the chapters of the book that give guidelines on how to use them. For instance, there is a short section on symbol accentuation as a method of teaching word recognition in the introduction, but this is elaborated and made clear with examples in Chapter 2: From Pictures to Print.

In teaching any individual child, it is very important to make what you do appropriate to his level. You may need to ask: can I start at all with my child (or pupil)? or do I need to do some preparation before taking even the first step? In Chapter 1, we set out checklists that help you to answer these questions.

In the following chapters, you will find ideas on how to help pupils bridge the gap between the recognition of pictures and the recognition of words; to build up a useful and extensive sight vocabulary; to group words into families and to recognize letters; to listen to and enjoy stories; to tell their own stories and to create their own reading matter; and to enjoy and use their recognition of printed words as seen in the environment of home and school and in books.

We know that our children can only go slowly on these paths to literacy. We think they can only do so with a lot of practice aimed at consolidating the learning. It is for this reason that we are eager to involve both teachers and parents in the children's education.

Indeed, a good way of using this book would be for teachers and parents to work from it together. For instance, the very necessary consolidation and "overlearning," often presented here in the form of games, could be used by teachers as "homework," in cooperation with parents. Parents are better placed to give a lot of attention to their own child when playing games at home. Teachers, on the other hand, with their greater trained skills, may be able to keep more detailed records of progress and coordinate this information with what the parents can give them. We give some ideas on how to do this in Chapter 9, "Recording Progress." Other ideas on parent and teacher involvement will be found in appropriate places in the text.

Terms Used in This Book

We are writing about young people who are very different from each other in their development. Some have "young" interests as well as a degree of intellectual development rather like that of young children. Others have very definite teenage pursuits and interests. Thus when we use the term "child," we have no particular age group in mind.

Also, we are thinking most of the time of parents as involved in the education of their children, and of teachers in the informal atmosphere of the special school as having mother-ly or fatherly roles. Hence "your child" can mean "child in the classroom" or "child in the family"; and "pupil" can mean the parent's pupil or the teacher's!

You will see that this does not lead to confusion in the text. When some adaptation is needed to put work into home or classroom, we give guidelines on how to go about it.

Finally, because it is inconvenient to keep saying "he" or "she," "him" and "her," we have used "he" and "him" throughout. But it must be understood that we have both sexes in mind!

IDEAS ABOUT READING

A bewildering amount has been written about reading—what it is, and how to teach it. There are reading schemes, sets of cards and kits, programs, ideas for getting children ready for reading, ideas for remedial work, tests for assessing reading competence, tests for diagnosing reading difficulties, surveys of standards in reading, general books evaluating approaches to reading; and some work on teaching word recognition to mentally handi-capped pupils, notably that of Gunzburg's *Social Sight Vocabu-larly* (1968).

There is no need to master all this, however interesting it may be, before beginning to teach an individual child to read. In fact, the ideas we are exploring in this book come from many sources but rely heavily on our own inventiveness and that of teachers and parents in response to individual children. We have, however, been strongly influenced by two approaches, ones we shall explain more fully in later chapters and illustrate as we go on. They are (1) symbol accentuation and (2) the language-experience approach. We describe these briefly below.

Symbol Accentuation

Before children can read print, they can usually recognize and see meaning in pictures. Reading is probably best thought of as a special form of language skill. One of the characteristics of human language is its symbolic nature: words, whether spoken or written, do not usually resemble the things or ideas they stand for. Thus the word "cup" in spoken or written form does not resemble the object for which it stands. This is quite unlike pictures or drawings. A picture of a cup, although it omits certain features of the real thing, does resemble it visually. So pupils who have reached the stage of "reading"—responding to pictures—need help before they can respond to words in print. Symbol accentuation is a way of bridging that gap. The word "cup" is presented so that it is not only like the world but also rather like a cup: $C\cup P$ —where we see the "u" is like a cup and the "p" is like its handle. This example comes from a paper by Miller and Miller (1968) in which they describe the method and their trial of it with handicapped pupils.

You will find more examples and guidelines on how to use and develop the idea in later chapters of this book (see Chapter 2, "From Pictures to Print"). We would like to emphasize that in our teaching of reading, we always recognize the importance of meaning. Symbol accentuation is one example of this early emphasis. We begin with the child's recognition of a cup, whether a picture or an object, and go to its written representation, first in the accentuated form and then in its normal spelling (traditional orthography).

The Language-Experience Approach

The language-experience approach rests on the idea of reading as a language skill. The best way to get the pupil into printed books, then, will be via the pupil's own language. The child will grasp language that reflects his own meanings better than the language in a book that some stranger thinks will interest all pupils of his age. But because natural language is partly developed and partly learned, the pupil's language experience will not be static. Language and experience will grow together. We concede that development is slower in mentally handicapped children and that sometimes it *seems* static, but there may be many reasons for this; we do not believe it is an unavoidable consequence of being mentally handicapped.

In the language-experience approach, the teacher or parent

will grasp this problem firmly and will give the child more language experience as well as introduce reading skills. A full description may be found in a book by Stauffer, *The Language-experience Approach to Reading* (1970). We also recommend a handy book by Gillham, *Teaching a Child to Read* (1976). However, for most purposes, teachers and parents will find enough in later chapters of this book to guide them in using this approach (see Chapter 4, "The Language-Experience Approach").

What Do We Mean by "Reading"?

In many books, "reading" is presented as a high mystery whose depths are hard to plumb and something that seems far removed from the powers and interests of the pupils we teach. Our view of "reading" is that it is a skill involving many preliminaries and related skills. Some aspects of what we are describing in this book may be thought of as prereading skills. After all, they are very similar to the activities that interested parents carry out in their own homes with children, both preschool and school age children—such things as telling stories and helping the child respond to picture books in the comfortable family atmosphere at bed time, participating in the child's games, and challenging the child. A lot of learning accrues from this, though the parents may not necessarily realize the helpful start the child is being given.

We know, also, how much better children do in school when this kind of involvement continues at home: many children already have some unsuspected word and letter recognition skills when they start school, skills acquired incidentally by frequent exposure to books and magazines.

This kind of experience has often not been available to mentally handicapped pupils, partly because of their slower development and attention difficulties.

Hence, in this book we present activities for you to use to help the child respond to pictures and stories, tell his own stories, draw pictures, and listen to someone reading aloud. The acquisition of a considerable Sight Vocabulary is an important

feature: the ability to recognize words in print that are meaning in speech.

With some pupils we may be able to proceed to reading
and responding to simple messages in print: creating simple
stories, having them written, and reading them back, aloud or
otherwise. All this is reading. Reading is not just being able to
read silently from a book. We do not know yet how far we can
go. We know from our experiment that it is possible to start
down this path, provided we use principles of learning and
teaching that derive from theory and good practice. In the next
section, we outline what we think these are.

IDEAS ABOUT LEARNING

An entire book could be written about learning. Some educators follow one theory wholeheartedly. We prefer a more
eclectic approach, adopting ideas that lead to successful practice. Our main question is: does it work? But that question
is more subtle than it appears. We break it down into other
questions:

Does the method (of teaching) work as economically as
possible? That is, with little waste of time?

Does the bit of learning contain the seeds of further learning? Does it allow us to go on, without first *un*learning?

Is it rewarding? That is, does it have some quality about it
now, some fun, some excitement, some challenge in and for
itself? We want to avoid the dull drills that are endurable only
because we hope they may pay off later. If the actual process
of learning is found by the pupil to be rewarding, the chances
are that he will "learn to learn." If not, he may well learn *not*
to learn!

In later chapters, you will find detailed examples of
methods that we believe lead to good results.

At this point we can sum up by offering five *principles*:

1. Have fun! The parent-child or teacher-pupil interaction should please
   both. In this book you will find examples of games that challenge
   the learner to think as well as to enjoy the experience.

2. Use the child's own strengths and initiatives. What can this child do well? What engages this child's attention? Start there.
3. Set realistic goals. It is important to recognize each small increment of learning and let the child know you have noticed it.
4. Consolidate the learning by
   (a) overlearning
   (b) learning to generalize
   (c) using well learned material in ever new and more challenging tasks and games.
   (d) revise.
5. Be ready to give the child a clue but fade this out as soon as possible. The child needs a crutch at first, but aim for it to be discarded.

None of the stated principles are special to handicapped children. In the next section, we consider mentally handicapped pupils as learners.

MENTALLY HANDICAPPED PUPILS AS LEARNERS

There is no doubt that mentally handicapped pupils are retarded in their development and that they develop slowly. Moreover, their developmental pattern (profile) is often uneven and more out-of-phase than that of "normal" pupils. However, it must be recognized that "normal" pupils also show out-of-phase development at times, notably at adolescence, when it is quite common to meet teenagers at puberty with incipient moustaches and breaking voices but still with the social and emotional development of children. In mentally handicapped pupils, the gaps are wider and more frequent.

Nevertheless, we deplore the idea that these pupils are so special that they must be taught by extraordinary methods or by different principles. The speed at which we move, the amount of help given, the achievement expected—this is what must be modified. The principles outlined above hold good for all pupils; the teacher or teaching parent of all pupils will be recognized as "good" for the same reasons—care in planning, mixed with sensitivity to the child's responses. Imagination and a sense of humor will also play a part.

Patterns of strengths and weaknesses are different among

individual mentally handicapped pupils, but we can make some acceptable general statements.

As pupils, they have some handicaps in learning: for instance, they tend to learn too specifically and do not generalize to new learning unless you help them. This can be done by consolidating and by applying old learning in new situations. They tend to be moody as learners, often shy and reluctant to start, especially if the situation is new to them: on some occasions, they work with enthusiasm, on others they reject everything. Parents and teachers need imagination and humor.

It is sometimes difficult to match their interest-age and their ability, especially when trying to get books and games for them. We have to plan for each individual, observing interests carefully. As the attention span may be limited, we have to find ways of catching and holding it.

However, as pupils, there are strengths. For instance, when they learn, they learn well and retain well, and they are usually, even at adolescence, without that infuriating spurious sophistication that can come between the average teenager in school and his parent or teacher.

Reading is a skill that makes demands on infant beginners. Is it an appropriate thing to demand of pupils with severe learning difficulties? We think it is for some of them.

HANDICAPPED PUPILS LEARNING TO READ

Schools for the handicapped differ from each other in the emphasis they put on teaching reading and writing. When children have severe learning difficulties, some educators argue that social and self-help skills should have a greater priority.

And with some children, of course, this will be so. Yet many of the skills they mean (such as the acquisition of some language) are in fact prerequisites for reading.

And for those who can acquire some reading ability, even if it is only the recognition of some words it seems wrong to deprive them of the opportunity to acquire it when we can think of ways to do it involving both teachers and parents.

Reading, at least in Western countries, is a skill acquired by most of the population: it is "normal" to be able to read. If handicapped teenagers can read on a level similar to those around them, it helps them to be accepted. It is part of social competence; it helps the teenager on the difficult path to independence. Your behavior is less dependent on others' spoken instructions if, for instance, you can read that the sign on that door or post-office position says "closed," or the words on the bottle of medicine say "for external use only." Besides being in one way a self-help skill, reading is a pleasure if even a small part of the world of story is opened up.

In the following chapters, we take into full account the problems that teaching reading to children with learning difficulties presents us with. We introduce practical notions of "What to do if . . ." to teachers and parents and describe certain methods in detail.

But as we also believe in freeing people to use their own ideas and adapt them to the individual way they are teaching, we also set our guidelines.

We begin with the checklists that help the teacher or parent find the pupil's level.

1

Readiness to read: finding the right level

INTRODUCTION

In our modern civilization reading is given a top priority. This has sometimes in the past been to the detriment of the slow learning pupil who has felt like a failure because efforts to teach him to read have in some cases not been successful—or in other cases all too successful—so that we have had children able to read mechanically, without any idea of what they are reading about.

Educators of mentally handicapped children have, quite rightly, reacted against this emphasis on the three Rs and have suggested that we should question our motives and get our priorities right. This revolution in the education of mentally handicapped children has been very beneficial. Instead of being helpless children looked after by adults, we see them becoming increasingly independent, walking confidently around the school, helping themselves at the table and serving others, talking to each other, learning to solve puzzles, learning to cook and do woodwork, to dance, to know about their own neighborhood, and to paint pictures and play act and go shopping.

By publishing a book called *Reading Is For Everyone*, it is in no way our intention to push the clock back, for we think that parent and teachers are getting their priorities right. Independence skills, communicative and social abilities, increased mobility and fine motor coordination, recreational skills, and artistic outlets are still our priorities. However, out of these, and particularly for teenagers, there *can* grow familiarity with the written word for many of these young people.

This will happen only if we match our teaching to the child's level of development—if we allow children to read at their own rate, if we introduce skills in carefully graded steps, and if we allow plenty of scope for practice and overlearning.

This familiarity with the written word will then widen the horizons of these young people. It will give them greater confidence and self-esteem, as well as increased independence and pleasure. We do not have to wait until we can read books out of the library before we can enjoy the written word. A child may get as much enjoyment out of reading his own name in print as we get from reading a novel.

Nor do we suggest that all mentally handicapped young people will eventually be able to read, even if given appropriate teaching. It is important that reading grows out of primary skills, so that if the child has not acquired these primary skills, the priority will be to help him to acquire them, rather than to embark on the teaching of reading. Thus, children represent their ideas and feelings through their play before they use language for this purpose; they understand spoken language before reading its representation in print; they recognize pictures or shapes before letters or words; they enjoy listening to nursery rhymes or jingles or stories before attempting to read them for themselves. Indeed, they must be able to recognize a sequence of real-life events before they can be expected to recognize a sequence of words, and most children have a store of well-understood first-hand experiences of ordinary living before they can accept the second-hand experience that is the subject matter of fiction.

If the child has not acquired these fundamental skills, we suggest you refer to two earlier books in this series: *Let Me Speak* and *Let Me Play*. They contain ideas on how to help the child to reach the point at which he is ready to begin the work in this book.

In this chapter, however, we offer some guidelines that will help you judge what level the child has reached and where to begin. The child's age will not help very much in making this decision. We have found in our research that some mentally handicapped teenagers are already reading and taking simple books out of the library, while others are not yet ready to begin with simple word recognition. Nevertheless, the method we explore in Chapter 2, "From Pictures to Print," enables us to begin to help pupils of low developmental levels to recognize words earlier than they would by more conventional methods. Normal three-and-a-half to four-year-olds enjoy this method and learn to recognize words by it and then, by the age of five or six, can go on to the language-experience approach in traditional orthography. But, remembering that there is an uneven profile of development in our children, we still consider that making a careful check on the child's behavior in various aspects of development will be necessary to help us decide what is appropriate for the child. At the end of this chapter, you will find checklists that can be used to both find an appropriate starting level and to chart the child's progress, once started.

Here are some guidelines to help you use these checklists. They can be used either by parents or by teachers, but preferably by home and school in cooperation.

GUIDELINES: USING THE CHECKLISTS TO FIND APPROPRIATE LEVELS

In order to gauge your child's readiness to begin to read, you need to find out the answers to these questions: At what level does he play? How much language can he respond to appropriately, and how much can he use? Does he understand pictures? Has he any elementary word recognition skills such as recognizing his own name?

The checklists provided list items in a sequence that is developmental; they go from easy to difficult. The topics of the checklists are those most directly concerned with prerequisites of reading, play, understanding of pictures and stories, use of language, understanding of language, and understanding of written instructions and signs.

In each checklist, there is a point marked where it would be appropriate for a child who has not yet begun to read to be started on the work in Chapter 2. Here is a summary of those points. They apply to most children.

CHECKLIST SUMMARY	ITEM
Play: engages in make-believe play involving a sequence of events, such as feeds doll, then washes it and puts it to bed, etc.; takes toy car from garage, goes shopping, brings car back. Uses imaginary objects.	7
Picture-books and stories: picks out details in pictures such as buttons on clothes, pens on table etc.	7
Understanding of language: can follow directions including the prepositions in and on, such as Put the toy in the box.	7
Use of language: uses mainly single words and short sentences; will respond both at home and in unfamiliar surroundings and be understood.	5
Written instructions and signs: recognizes his own name written down.	5

Some Exceptions

Suppose your child achieves the appropriate level on some checklists, but not on others. For instance, some mentally handicapped children have specific difficulty in either the understanding or the use of spoken language. With these children, it is often necessary to try an alternative form of communication that does not rely upon the spoken word, such as Bliss symbols or Paget-Gorman.*

Such children can actually be helped to extend their understanding of language by the symbol accentuation method

*See *Stimulating the Exceptional Child* by Chris Kiernan, Jordan, and Chris Saunders, Prentice-Hall, 1984.

of word-recognition. But they do constitute a special case. For most children, no attempt should be made to start on the reading scheme until the level of understanding of language indicated in item 7 in the charts is reached. Even with those exceptional children, their level of play should be the appropriate one.

The last item, "recognizes own name," although desirable, is not absolutely essential if other achievements are right. In our own experiment, we were able to teach children successfully who had not yet learned to recognize their own name. But they had reached appropriate points on the other checklists.

FILLING IN THE CHECKLISTS

Fill in the charts carefully and honestly. It is harmful to the child's progress to overestimate or underestimate his achievements. Check each item that you consider your child *regularly* achieves on his own with encouragement, but not direct help. For instance, we have found it useful to watch a child's spontaneous self-initiated activity, such as his play.

Do not interfere with this activity or you will not get a true reading of his development. Just hand him appropriate toys and be *generally* supportive and watch what he does with them, or watch him throughout a day.

You will find the appropriate activity for your child indicated in the last column of the checklist. If he is still at an earlier stage of play than the one we need to start this book, you will find ideas for raising his level in the earlier book *Let Me Play* in this series.

Similarly, give him plenty of opportunity to respond to different stories in picture books. An important introduction to reading is fostered by an early familiarity and love of books. We offer (see Chapter 6) a list of books to read from, and suggest some ideas for fostering the art of listening and looking at picture books. Hence, if your child does not yet reach the appropriate level for beginning word recognition, we direct you to Chapter 6 and the list on page 145.

When evaluating the child's understanding of language, you

will need to give instructions to see if the child responds. Try not to give clues by gesture or looking in the right direction. Be cautious in crediting a child with use of language items. Here it may be especially important for teacher and parent to check each other's checklist! If the child is not at the appropriate level on these two checklists, he can be helped by referring to an earlier book in this series, *Let Me Speak*, as we indicate in the final column in the checklists.

Finally, for the checklist Written Instructions and Signs, you will need to develop little tasks to see if he can do what the item suggests. You can use household objects for sorting, such as buttons and beads. Say things like "Find all the buttons"; "Give me the red circles"; "What's this?"; or you can present four pictures of common objects and say "Show me the chair."

If your child cannot do the first three items on the checklist, he will be directed to *Let Me Play*; but there are many suggestions in Chapter 3 of this book for improving his ability with the later items. You will find in all the checklists that Chapter 2 and 6 appear many times, whereas Chapters 7 and 8 are advised only when children have developed the skills promoted in the earlier chapters. This is because Chapter 2 shows how to teach new words whenever this is necessary; and Chapter 6 fosters interest in books and keeps up motivation.

USING THE CHECKLISTS
TO CHART PROGRESS

In filling in the checklists, it is important to remember that we are attempting to help the child move to the next stage on the chart. We should work at the stage he is *at* and enrich it, over-learn it in fact, by all kinds of varied practice—using games and activities many times. Not until he is *absolutely* competent should we attempt to move on. By filling in these checklists at intervals very carefully and cautiously, you will be able to keep a record of your child's progress in the acquisition of pre-reading and reading skills. (For a finer graded recording of these, see the suggestions in Chapter 9).

But these are not the only developments you will be

recording. For instance, as your child plays the games to help him recognize words, he will also be learning *how* to play those games—an important social skill in its own right. As he listens to stories or makes his own books, he will have more opportunities of learning language. It will be interesting to record his progress in these areas as well as in reading.

CHECKLIST 1: PLAY

	Check box, if child achieves item *regularly*	Suggested chapter
1. Treats all toys alike, banging or mouthing or feeling them.	☐	
2. Shows some differentiation in his treatment of toys: will shake a rattle or hit a drum but not the other way round.	☐	
3. Relational play; will put objects in a box or pile one brick on another.	☐	
4. Begins to treat toys according to their use: will comb hair with toy comb, push a car along, pretend to drink from a toy cup.	☐	
5. Engages in simple pretend play: feeds a doll briefly with a toy spoon, kisses and hugs stuffed animal.	☐	
6. Engages in make-believe play: puts a doll to bed, uses a box as a car, washes doll.	☐	Chapter 6 (Picture books) Chapter 2 (From Pictures to Print) using pictures only Chapter 4 simple games
7. Engages in make-believe play involving a sequence of events such as feeds doll then washes it and puts it to bed. Takes toy car from garage, goes to the store, comes back to garage. Uses imaginary objects.	☐	
8. Engages in role play, pretending to be a postman or doctor etc. Calls people on toy phone.	☐	
9. More elaborate role play involving other people in co-operative effort.	☐	Chapter 2 symbol accentuation Chapter 4 more elaborate games Chapter 6
10. Plays games with rules, such as "Tag" or "Hide-and-seek."	☐	

CHECKLIST 1: PLAY (continued)

	Check box, if child achieves item *regularly*	Suggested chapter
11. Plays table games, e.g., "Snap," "Dominoes."	☐	Chapter 2 & 3 & 4
12. Plays more elaborate table games such as "Checkers" or "Sorry."	☐	*Only* proceed to chapter 7 when chapter 4 is completed. Chapter 6

Child should achieve item 7 before beginning Chapter 2 in this book.

CHECKLIST 2: PICTURE BOOKS AND STORIES

	Check box, if child achieves item *regularly*	Suggested chapter
1. Recognizes a few pictures of objects.	☐	
2. Listens to a short story about a picture.	☐	
3. Turns over the pages of a picture book.	☐	
4. Recognizes familiar people in photographs.	☐	Chapter 6
5. Identifies seven pictures of common objects.	☐	
6. Uses actions with pictures, for example, pretends to feed picture of doll.	☐	
7. Picks out details in pictures, such as buttons on clothes, pen on table, etc.	☐	Chapter 2, 5 and 6
8. Listens eagerly to stories told from picture books and likes to have them read over and over again.	☐	
9. Remembers some of the words of familiar stories or rhymes and will join in when they are read to him.	☐	Chapters 2, 4, 5, 6
10. Memorizes simple stories and rhymes and will "read" them from memory on his own.	☐	Chapters 2, 3, 4, 5, 6

Child should achieve item 7 before beginning Chapter 2.

CHECKLIST 3: UNDERSTANDING OF LANGUAGE

	Check box, if child achieves item *regularly*	Suggested chapter
1. Responds to words—looks around when asked "Where's Daddy."	☐	
2. Points to familiar person or toy when asked.	☐	
3. Understands when told *not* to do something.	☐	
4. Points to five parts of doll or person when asked to point out hair, eyes, nose, mouth, hands.	☐	
5. Responds to two or three directions, such as "Get your coat."	☐	
6. Can get one object from another room without forgetting.	☐	
7. Can follow directions including the prepositions **in** and **on** such as, "Put the toy **in** the box."	☐ ⎫	
8. Will get several objects from another room without forgetting.	☐ ⎭	Chapters 2 and 6
9. Follows two-part instructions, such as "Go downstairs and look for the mail." "Pick up your sweater and put it on the hanger."	☐	Chapters 2, 5, 6
10. Can remember simple instructions and reliably carry them out later, such as messages from school or work.	☐ ⎫	
11. Can remember and carry out a sequence of instructions, such as a simple recipe or directions to a place.	☐ ⎭	Chapters 2, 3, 4, 5, 6

Child should achieve item 7 before beginning Chapter 2.

CHECKLIST 4: USE OF LANGUAGE (EXPRESSIVE LANGUAGE)

	Check box, if child achieves item *regularly*	Suggested chapter
1. Responds to cuddling and attention with vocalizations.	☐	
2. Uses a few gestures to make wants known and some idiosyncratic articulations. Can be understood only by family and friends.	☐	
3. Uses mainly gestures to make wants known, both at home and in unfamiliar surroundings. Uses a few words and is quite good at being understood at a simple level.	☐	
4. Uses mainly single words or short sentences but can be understood by family and friends—not always by strangers.	☐	
5. Uses single words and short sentences and will respond both at home and in unfamiliar surroundings and be understood. Gives own name and address.	☐	Chapters 2, 5, 6
6. Expressive language good but not always appropriate. Response to others and to the situation limited.	☐	
7. Uses appropriate language in day-to-day situations and responds to others both at home and in unfamiliar surroundings. Cannot always be clearly understood because of poor articulation.	☐	Chapters 2, 4, 5, 6
8. Can be clearly understood by others and uses appropriate language in all day-to-day situations both at home and in unfamiliar surroundings. Able to give and receive information and retell the events of the day.	☐	Chapters 2, 3, 4, 5, 6

Child should achieve item 5 before beginning Chapter 2.

CHECKLIST 5: WRITTEN INSTRUCTION AND SIGNS

	Check box, if child achieves item *regularly*	Suggested chapter
1. Sorts out objects.	☐	
2. Matches by color, distinguishes red circles from green circles.	☐	
3. Sorts out shapes, such as circles from squares.	☐	
4. Identifies pictures of common objects.	☐	Chapter 6
5. Recognizes own name written down.	☐	
6. Recognizes record covers and can pick out his own favorites reliably.	☐	Chapters 2, 3, 5, 6
7. Recognizes a few familiar names or words, such as mother.	☐	
8. Recognizes one or two labels in kitchen, such as rice and sugar.	☐	
9. Recognizes and picks out trade names in supermarkets, such as Tide or Ivory.	☐	Chapters 2, 3, 5, 6
10. Recognizes more than 6 labels on cans and bottles.	☐	
11. Recognizes and *acts appropriately* to signs, such as **Ladies, Gentlemen, Danger, Walk, Bus stop, Exit, Entrance, On,** and **Off.**	☐	

	Check box, if child achieves item *regularly*	Suggested chapter
12. Can read and *react appropriately* to signs giving directions in stores, home, street, etc., such as Elevator out of order, This way up, Employees only, pay here.	☐	Chapters 2, 3, 4, 5, 6
13. Can read and follow a line of instructions, such as Cut along dotted line, To call operator lift hand set.	☐	Chapters 7 and 8, with occasional returns to Chapter 2 to teach unknown words. Chapter 6 for reading experience.
14. Can read and follow a sequence of instructions, such as a recipe, a knitting pattern, or a direction on a packet.	☐	
15. Can read a simple book for pleasure. Takes books out of library.	☐	

Note on Checklist 5

The recognition of written instructions and signs is important for independence, and this checklist will be helpful in gauging your child's level of independence in this way. However, there are other aspects of independence.

Nevertheless, if your child can recognize pictures and his own name, it will be possible to begin the activities described in Chapters 2 and 3, "From Pictures to Print" and "Recognizing every-day words."

2

From pictures to print

INTRODUCTION

It took mankind thousands of years before people were able to use a sophisticated method of sending messages in writing. First they had to get used to picture writing and ascribe meanings to marks on paper or scratches in stone. Then, gradually, the pictures became less like real objects and actions or ideas and it took even longer before signs began to be associated with *sounds* instead of with whole words. Even so, until the late nineteenth century writing was not a skill available to most adults: in ancient civilizations, writing and reading were in the hands of a few learned men in the service of kings.

Yet, we expect children to go through this process, that took civilization so long, in a few years. They have first to learn to recognize objects, then learn their names, then learn the many different ways of depicting them. Once they are able to do this, we expect them to start recognizing at least a few words. Because children generally make this step without much trouble, and because we usually forget our own early experiences, we may not realize how big and mysterious a step this is.

Let us try to put ourselves in the child's shoes

Can you
read this?

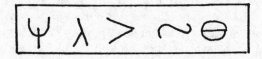

or this?

Of course you cannot, because we have made up our own
alphabet. However, if we drew this 🏠 and this
🐎 you would have no difficulty. Yet we have given you
an easier task than we give children when they are learning to
read, because you already know that letters stand for sounds,
that you read from left to right, and that groups of letters make
words. You also know that as these two words have many
letters in common, they must be similar words. Many children
take this step from pictures to print quite easily but others do
not, and the more we try to get them to *read* the more bemused
they become. Also, because we find it hard to conceal our dis-
appointment, they are in danger of feeling like complete
failures. They may not be able to express their feelings very well
and may become depressed, uncooperative, or naughty.

Teachers find that the children who seem to have very
little difficulty in school usually have had a great deal of help
from their parents before they come to school. We do not mean
that their parents have set out to be "teachers," but rather that
the parents have played with their children a lot and, without
knowing it, have laid the foundations for reading and writing.

Particularly, these parents have sat down with their children and a picture book, perhaps every evening.

It is easy to see how the picture book leads the child into words. Under the pictures there will be captions and the parents will read these: "That says 'Three Blind Mice.'" Nearly always the child will have a favorite picture book and will insist on looking at this time and time again. Gradually he will be telling *you* what the words say under each picture. You may tease him by reading them wrong, and he will indignantly correct you. He is half way to being able to read.

Later the child may insist on a bed-time story every night. Some parents read these and some make them up—perhaps about the child himself. These stories are important because they whet the child's appetite for more stories, which one day he can read himself from books.

He may play with alphabet blocks. When he is very small, they are fun to build with and to knock over. But in the game, a parent may also say "That A is for apple, B for banana," and these names will stick in the child's mind.

Or parents may play games like "I spy" with their children. This game draws the child's attention to the initial letter sounds of words in a playful way. Listen to a family playing such a game. At first the youngest member is helped with a word, but as he grows older he begins to understand the game and can play properly.

Nursery rhymes and nonsense rhymes recited by parents and grandparents to the child from babyhood are excellent practice in listening to sounds.

So you see there is a folk wisdom in all these games. Not only do they knit the family together, they also help the child to learn painlessly, without knowing he is learning. This is the best way of learning because the child is always in the position of wanting to do it.

However, what about the child who, because of some handicap, is not ready to learn to read until he is much older? We may have given up hope before he was mature enough to benefit from these games, so he missed out on them. Now he seems too old for such childish play.

In this chapter we shall outline ways in which parents and teachers of handicapped children can help them take this next step in an enjoyable way and bridge the gap from pictures to print.

In no way should these ideas be treated as a "lesson." You will find that these games will enrich the family life if they are treated as fun.

Very importantly, no notice should be taken if a child makes a mistake or takes longer than you expect to grasp the idea. We have tried to ensure that every child will have success at each stage, so long as you choose an appropriate game and do not try to be too ambitious.

The games we shall describe are suitable for a young person who is able to recognize at least ten pictures, and either name them or pick them out from a display when you say, for instance, "Find the ball."

The child is then ready to bridge the gap from pictures to print.

First let us think about why a picture is easy to recognize and a word is not.

STEP 1.   GUESS WHAT I'M DRAWING?

How Soon Can You Guess?

Take a pile of index cards and a pencil and tell your child you are going to draw a picture on each, and see how soon he can guess what it is you are drawing. You do not have to be an artist to do this. In fact the simpler the picture the better. Here are some examples.

Make sure you choose pictures he will know—do not be too ambitious and try drawing violins or zebras! Make it simple and add extra details only if necessary.

To make the game more fun, let the child make a pile of all the pictures he has guessed correctly. At the end of the game you can count how many he has in the pile and praise him. If this is not a sufficient reward you can give him something extra for each picture he guesses such as a piece of candy or something else he likes. If he guesses wrong and calls a hat a cake, accept his version if it is reasonable, otherwise put the picture aside and name it yourself.

What about the child who has speech difficulties so that his speech is unintelligible? There is no reason why he should not play this game—in fact it may help him considerably. But you will have to devise a different version for him. As well as the cards that you are going to draw on, you will need a collection of small objects or colored pictures. When you draw a cat, for instance, he must find a model cat, or point to the colored picture of a cat, to win. Also, try to get him to name the picture as well as he can.

Take Turns

Once your child has understood the game and enjoys it, you should try taking turns and let *him* be the artist while you guess. Never mind if the pictures are pretty hard to guess. Your child will learn a lot by instructing you.

Before going on to the next stage, play more games at this stage. (See page 6).

STEP 2. GUESS WHAT I'M DRAWING NOW?

This is a more difficult guessing game, but it is played in just the same way as Step 1. You may need a little practice before playing it and quite a lot of ingenuity because you are going to incorporate the letters of a word into your picture in such a way that the child's attention is drawn to each letter. We shall give you some examples, but then you will have to devise some of your own as well, because individual children have different interests. Here is a simple one:

Now you must not *tell* your child what you are drawing: it is a guessing game, so *he* has to tell you. But you can give him as many clues as he needs—"It says meow," "It purrs." (Don't give him extra clues if he does *not* need them.)

It is important, as you draw, to focus his attention on the letter shapes. Say something like this: "See if you can guess what I am drawing. It is an animal. . . , This is its head."

On the next page are more examples to get you started. (Further examples of pictures, symbol accentuation and traditional orthography will be found at the end of the chapter.)

The clues you give are very important because you want to arrange it so that your child guesses correctly. If by chance he does *not* guess correctly, put that drawing aside, if possible without letting him see it and start another

Remember not to say the word before your child does.

Do not be too ambitious, and draw only three of these word pictures to start with—repeat the same pictures if you like.

These word pictures are called symbol accentuated words—

SAW for short. We will use this abbreviation throughout the rest of the text.

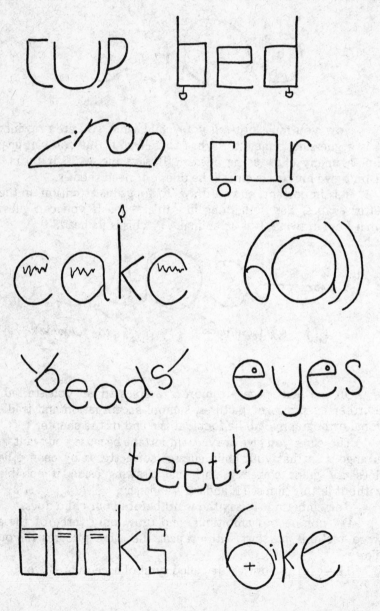

toes   *dOg*

Words that have not been made into pictures are said to be written in traditional orthography (TOW—traditional orthography words).

Once your child has recognized three SAWs, play lots of games with them (for games, see the next part of this chapter and Chapter 5). This is important, as your child needs to over-learn each step to the point at which he is so familiar with the words that you cannot catch him, however hard you try. Games are the best way of ensuring this.

STEP 3.   THE BRIDGE

Building a bridge from a picture word (SAW) to a printed word (TOW) is the hardest part of this process and has to be introduced carefully. There are two ways of doing this. We shall describe the simplest method first. If this does not work, you may have to resort to the second method.

Method 1.   Quick Flip

Tell your child you are going to play a harder guessing game. Pick out a SAW card that he already knows very well, and on the back of it write the same word in TOW. As before, write it slowly letter by letter and give clues to ensure success.

Here is an example:

"See if you can guess what I am drawing. I will make it harder. It is an animal. . . .

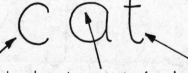

here's its head   here's its back   here's its funny tail.
                                          its rather short

What is it?"

If your child is not sure, let him have a "quick flip" to the other side of the card where the picture word (SAW) is drawn.

Do this with the three picture words (SAW) he already knows.

You will now have three cards. Each will have a word printed in ordinary print on one side and the same word made into a picture on the reverse side.

It may take a lot of practice before your child knows the words in ordinary print for certain without the help of the picture words. He will need to play lots of games with these before you go on to the next step. Whatever game you choose, never allow the child to flounder. If he is not certain, let him have a "quick flip" and look at the other side, which he already knows.

Method 2. Fading It Out

Some children find it difficult to jump straight from the picture word to the word in ordinary print. This method helps them, by reducing the number of clues gradually.

Stage 1. For example, on the back of the picture word card, draw the following:

Stage 2. Draw the picture word again but without distorting the letters so much:

Play games with this side uppermost, and, if necessary, let your child have a quick flip to the other side.

When he is recognizing these cards without having to flip them over, go on to Stage 3:

Prepare another set of cards with Stage 2 on one side and ordinary print on the other. See if he can recognize the ordinary print, but if he has any difficulty let him flip the card over as before. Again play plenty of games with these cards.

THE WORD BANK

Once your child is able to name and recognize a few word cards, whether in picture words (SAW) or ordinary print (TOW), give him a box or file to keep them in. Do not let him add any to his collection until you are sure that he knows them well: that is,

1. he can name the words on three separate occasions without prompting;
2. he can pick out the words on three separate occasions from a display of four different words without prompting.

This word bank is important. Not only does it give the child a sense of achievement, but it also gives you a record of progress. (If you want to, pencil in the date when each word qualifies to be added to the bank). At a later date, further learning can be based on this bank.

MORE WORDS

Once the child has grasped the idea of the word game, new word pictures should be introduced. But—a word of warning. You may be tempted to go too fast at this stage. Try to resist, as failure can easily upset a child's confidence. One, two, or three words are enough to introduce at one time.

Be guided in your choice of new words by the child himself. He may be able to suggest what he would like you to draw. He is much more likely to remember the word if he suggested it in the first place. At this stage it will be best to stick to words which are nouns (names of common objects).

As soon as possible include the child's own name among the picture words if he does not already recognize it. Here is an example of turning a name into a picture:

With each word you introduce, go through all the stages as before, and, as the word bank gets bigger, games can be played with all the cards together. This will ensure revision.

Warning Note

The more words a child learns, the more difficult it may be for him to distinguish between them. Do not be disappointed if he begins to fail where he succeeded earlier. Backtrack and play some more games with the old words.

OTHER WORDS

A child does not need to be able to recognize only labels of things. He also has to recognize other words: words denoting actions (verbs—eat, sleep); describing words (adjectives—big, little, red); words showing positions (prepositions—up, down, in); and words that describe how an action is done (adverbs—quickly, slowly).

There are, of course, other parts of speech in the English language, but we will leave learning these until later. The words listed above cannot all easily be drawn as picture words. Here are some other ways of introducing them.

Verbs (Action Words)

Some of these can be turned into picture words. Here are some examples:

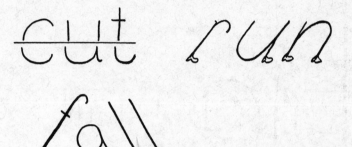

Others do not lend themselves easily to this treatment. This is what you can do with the word **jump**.

Write **jump** on a card in ordinary print. Ask your child to guess what the card is doing while you jump the card up and down in front of him. You may also have to add an arrow to the card—**jump** so that he still recognizes it when it is not moving, and then gradually fade out this extra clue.

Adverbs

With adverbs like **fast** or **slow**, you can also use movement to help your child to guess.

Adjectives

Colors—print the word in its own color on one side of the card and in black on the other.

Examples of other adjectives:

big

little

cold

wet

tall

long

Prepositions

Here are some examples.

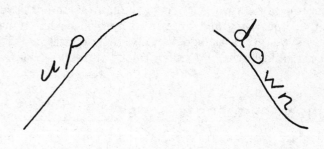

(These are a bit harder)

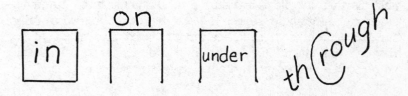

By now you will be able to be more inventive, and introduce the words that interest your own child. You may also find that very little accentuation is needed even for new words. This is fine, never use more than you need. Eventually you will not need any at all. However, try not to confine the accentuation to one letter only, as this may lead to problems later on. Get your child to pay attention to all the letters in a word, not just to the first.

PUTTING TWO WORDS TOGETHER

Once your child has a collection of words in his word bank, you can try putting two of them together, such as **big cat**. You may be inclined to assume that if he can read **big** and **cat** he can automatically put them together into a phrase and read **big cat**. This is not necessarily so. It is quite a big step from recognizing single words to recognizing phrases, and the child may need plenty of practice.

Once a child can do this, he can have plenty of fun making new phrases of his own, such as **big cup, little cup,** or **little cat.** Do not be too hasty and jump in if he makes some nonsense phrases as well, such as **big Joan, cup little** or **wet dry.** This is the way a child learns—by trying things out and seeing if they work.

PUTTING MORE WORDS TOGETHER

At this stage, you can help a child to realize that he can put more than two words together and make sense. Do not worry if these words do not form a complete sentence and are rather telegraphic, such as **Joan jump out, little red cat, big fast car.** Just as when a child is learning to speak, he has to go through a stage of telegraphic speech before he can cope with fully formed sentences, a child learning to read also needs to go through this stage. Once your child is competent at this level, go on to the next section: the language-experience approach.

WORD MEANING

Once your child has a repertoire of words that he can recognize, introduce some variations to keep him on his toes. Instead of laying out a display of words he knows and asking him to find the one that says **cat** or **house,** for instance, try displaying them in the same way and asking him to find the one that ''meows'' or the one ''we live in.'' This kind of variation will insure against automatic responses and will keep up interest during practice.

GAMES TO PLAY

Introduction

Crossing the bridge from no word recognition to the recognition of a dozen or so words in TO may take quite a long time. In our experience with teenagers, this took more than six months to accomplish. However, it would be counter-productive to try to hurry this stage, as it is a very fundamental one. Indeed, if you are to be successful, every little step has to be consolidated and over-learned. The student must feel the assurance that is gained from absolute confidence in his ability. Once this is achieved, he will be ready to take the next step. However, this confidence and overlearning will not be helped by boring and monotonous repetition. It *will* be helped by various games around the same theme. At each step, a variety of games should be played and repeated. If your student suggests a game or varies the rules, you will know that, even in a limited way, he is motivated to help his own learning. This is a very important landmark with young people who are not noted for taking the initiative. If you find your pupil floundering at any point, backtrack to an easier stage.

Another important thing to remember is that "a little and often" is much more effective than infrequent long sessions. Half an hour or even a quarter of an hour playing a game each day will be most helpful. Another thing to remember is that once the games have been established, you can recruit grand-parents, sisters, brothers, friends, and neighbors to play them with your pupil. However, *you* will need to be the one who helps your pupil take the next step forward.

THE GAMES

1. Who Can Find It First?

This game can be played from Step 1, but you can start playing it at Step 2 and Step 3.

Materials. Separate cards either with pictures (Step 1) or symbol accentuated words (Step 2) or words in ordinary print (Step 3).

Method. Lay the cards face-up on the table or floor and tell your child you are going to have a race to find a card. Name a card and see if your child can pick it out. Do not let him get there first every time, but let him have more success than failure. You can vary this game by hiding the cards around the room so that he has to search. This will help his memory span.

At first, he may forget what he is looking for before he has found it. Gradually increase the length of time he has to spend searching.

2.   Shoot It Down

Other pupils, especially boys, seem to enjoy this game, but it is not suitable for all pupils, as it does require considerable hand-eye coordination.

Materials.   Large cards with either pictures (Step 1), SA words (Step 2) or TO words (Step 3) printed on them.

A piece of wood shaped like a gun with an elastic band stretched over it so that it can be shot off.

A table.

Method.   The cards are propped up at the back of a table against the wall in such a way that they fall down behind the table if hit. The pupil stands behind the table and aims at a card. Depending on how good a shot he is, he either names the card he is aiming at or the one he has just hit.

3.   Roll and Stop

Materials.   A set of cards as before, either pictures (Step 1) or SA words (Step 2), or TO words (Step 3), are placed one above the other at the right hand side of a table.

A wooden or cardboard ramp (not too steep).

A matchbox car. A box to provide a barrier.

Method.   The pupil names a target word or picture and tries to roll the car down the ramp so that it stops at the right word. The box at the end of the row ensures that the car does not roll off the table or to a spot that is not opposite any word. If the car stops opposite the wrong word, the pupil has to name this word or picture.

More energetic variations of this game with larger words or pictures can be placed on the floor, and a ball can be used instead of a car.

Activity seems to aid learning, and, if your pupil is rather passive it is a good idea to involve him in a more energetic game.

4. Find the Pair

This is a traditional game and is good for increasing the memory span.

Materials. Pairs of cards with either pictures (Step 1) or SA words (Step 2), or TO words (Step 3) printed on them.

Method. The cards are placed face down on the table in a random order, and each player has to turn one card without moving it from its position on the table and then try to make a pair by turning another card over.

If the two upturned cards make a pair the player claims them for his own. If they do not, he turns them back and the next player takes his turn. At the end of the game each player counts how many pairs he has.

5. Poke It Through

Materials. For this game you have to prepare a large card with holes punched in it large enough to put a pencil through. On one side of the card you print a suitable series of pictures or picture words or printed words that the pupil knows; under each picture there is a hole. On the other side the same words are printed over the appropriate holes.

Method. The teacher sits on the printed side of the card and reads out a word. The pupil has to stick his pencil through the appropriate hole.

6. Bingo

There are many versions of this game and it can be adapted to meet individual needs. Here is the basic game.

Materials. A set of cards marked out into six squares or rectangles. In each square there is a picture, SAW, or TOW printed. A set of little cards the same size as one of the squares on the big card, with the same pictures, SAWs, or TOWs printed on them.

Method.   The dealer holds up a little card and the other players have their marked out cards in front of them. The players then name the card that has been held up and claim it if it matches one of theirs. They can then cover the appropriate picture with the card or a square of paper. The winner is the one who covers all the spaces on the card first.

It is best to start with an easy version of this game before making it more exacting:

> *Stage 1*   The dealer holds up a picture card and the player claims it if he has the same picture on his card. (All picture cards.)
>
> *Stage 2*   The dealer calls out a word from a card and the player claims it if he has a picture to match. (Word cards for the dealer—picture for the player.)
>
> *Stage 3*   The dealer displays a printed word and the player claims it if he has a printed word to match on his card. (All printed words for player and dealer in SA or TO.)
>
> *Stage 4*   The dealer calls out a word and the player claims it if he has a printed word to match on his card. (All printed words for player and dealer in SA or TO.)

STAGE 4 BINGO

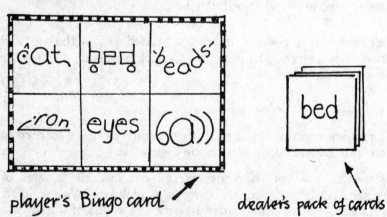

player's Bingo card   dealer's pack of cards

Note: Although this game can be played at any stage, it is particularly appropriate when the pupil has 12 or more words in his word bank, as it serves as revision.

7. Snap

Materials.   A set of cards has to be prepared with at least four copies of each word or picture. Playing cards can be used with a piece of plain paper taped to cover the face, with the picture or word drawn on it.

Method.   Deal out the cards. Each player puts one down in front of him in turn.

When two identical cards appear the first player to call out their name claims his opponent's pile of cards and puts them with the ones of his own that are on the table on the back of his pack. The player who finishes with all the cards in his pack is the winner.

8. Dominoes

Materials.   A set of dominoes has to be made with pictures, picture words, or printed words instead of dots. If necessary, reduce the number of dominoes in the set at first. Dominoes can be made out of stiff cardboard, plywood, or matchboxes.

Method.   Play like conventional dominoes. Deal the dominoes around and take turns to place a domino against one that matches. Once your student has grasped the rules of the game, introduce a new rule, such as you can only place your domino if you can name it first.

WORDS IN PRINT

Once your child can recognize a few words, keep a look out for these words in print (in newspapers, magazines, or books).

See if he can find, or recognize, the word on the printed page.

You will have to help at first, perhaps by underlining the word.

There will also be difficulty in recognizing unfamiliar print. This is one of the difficulties in generalization that mentally handicapped children have.

BOOKS

A child's first book will be a picture book with pictures of common objects on each page. The very best first book is one that has been made specially for one particular child. Then the pictures can be directly related to the child's life and interests. As soon as the young person is recognizing a few words, a book should be made with these words in it (one to a page).

Short books are better than long ones at this stage, as the child can see his achievement if he first reads one book and then two and so on. Illustrating each page should not be difficult. Either the child can illustrate them himself, if he is able, or *you* can illustrate them for him. At the end of the book, list the words and see whether your child can read them without the help of the pictures.

A good idea, for the first few books anyway, is to make a card duplicate for each word in the book, then stick an envelope at the bottom of each page and keep the words in these.

Sometimes, take all the words out of the envelopes and mix them up. See if your child can put them back in the right places. At first, let him match them with the word on the printed page. Later, cover this word up and see if he can match the pictures to the words.

MAKING A START

Once you have made a start, you should have no difficulty in accentuating words. But, in our experience, parents and teachers feel that this is beyond them at first and are reluctant to begin. They often attempt much more elaborate accentuation than is necessary. For this reason, we have included some pages of illustrations to get you started. Each word is represented by a picture and a symbol accentuated picture and is also printed in TO. The pictures have been drawn quite large and can be traced or copied larger to make cards.

THE ALPHABET

Recognition of the individual letters in the alphabet is much more difficult than we usually realize, although it is introduced to children very early in life through alphabet blocks and books.

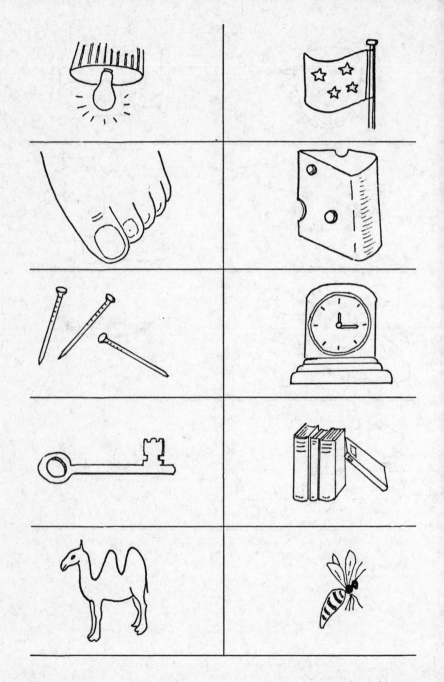

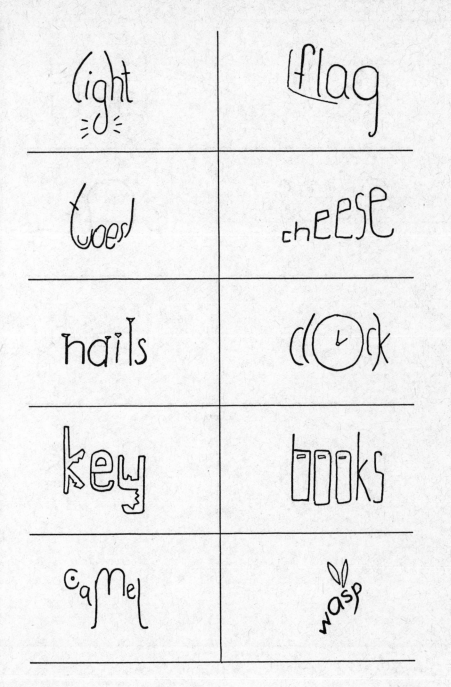

light

flag

toes

cheese

nails

clock

key

books

camel

wasp

cup	bed
eyes	cat
shoe	teeth
train	mouse

cup	bed
eyes	cat
shoe	teeth
train	mouse

light	flag
toes	cheese
nails	clock
key	books
camel	wasp

We can best appreciate how difficult it is by trying to learn the Greek or Russian alphabet later in life, or even the Morse Code. It is quite a strain on the memory.

For children, there is an added difficulty. Up to this point, they have learned that it does not matter which way up an object is a pipe is still a pipe when it is upside down. However, if a letter is upside down, it is no longer the same letter—an upside down *p* for instance becomes a *d* and so on. This is very confusing. Also, in the written word, letter order becomes important and the word *saw* becomes *was* if the order is reversed. In most practical aspects of life, the exact order does not matter: We still have the same groceries, whatever order we buy them in.

This suggests that we have to be very cautious as to *how* and *when* we teach a child his letters.

How to Introduce the Alphabet

A young child or a developmentally immature child does not think like an adult. His thinking is not abstract and logical but imaginative and pictorial. If we introduce the alphabet first in an imaginative and pictorial way, a young child will be able to relate to it without strain, and this is what we are going to suggest. First, the shape of each letter will be linked with a picture of an object that starts with that letter, and this connection will be firmly established before new words are introduced. Second, we will introduce letter sounds only in the context of whole words. Progress will be from a meaningful and familiar *complete* unit—the word—towards a growing familiarity with the components of that unit—the letters.

To introduce letter sounds in isolation at this stage would lead to confusion, and even at a later stage should be avoided as much as possible. It is almost impossible to sound out a single consonant—*b,c,d,f*—without distorting it with an additional vowel sound—*a,e,i,o,u*.

We suggest that whole words be introduced first by means of symbol accentuation. It is not necessary to learn the individual letters until your child has learned to recognize at least twenty of these.

The child will then have had some practice in sorting words out in his word bank and putting them back in the appropriate sections by means of the letter dividers.

Once he has reached this stage, you can begin to introduce the pictorial alphabet as a *separate* activity, but do not be in too great a hurry. If there is any danger of this confusing him, leave it until later.

How to Make a Pictorial Alphabet

In this chapter we will give you an example of a pictorial alphabet that you can trace or copy (see end of chapter). However, it will probably be much more effective if you make your own to suit the individual student. You do not have to be a great artist to do this; just use a little imagination.

We used a piece of stiff paper or cardboard measuring ten inches by fourteen inches. We marked it in rectangles measuring one and a half inches by two inches with half-inch spaces in between. This made five rectangles in each row, and five complete rows, with one rectangle in the last row, for the twenty-six letters of the alphabet. A separate covering flap (one and a half inches by two inches) was made for each letter.

Each letter was printed in both upper and lower case on each flap and the pictorial version of the letters were drawn underneath on the sheet of card (see page 54).

How to Use the Pictorial Alphabet

The best way to use the alphabet is to introduce it in the form of a repetitive story that introduces one letter at a time and builds as it goes along. It does not have to be an elaborate story. It can be a simple narrative of events, perhaps using the child as the chief character. For instance you can begin by turning only one flap back, revealing the picture of the apple. You then start the story of *Mary* who went for a walk and saw something lying on the grass underneath a tree. When she came up to it she saw it was an apple and she picked it up and took it home. Or it could be a story of *John* who went shopping for his mother who wanted some apples, so he went down Main Street until he saw an apple in the shop window and then went

in to buy some. When you have finished this, you turn down
the flap and hide the *apple* and see if your student can find it
again.

PICTORIAL ALPHABET

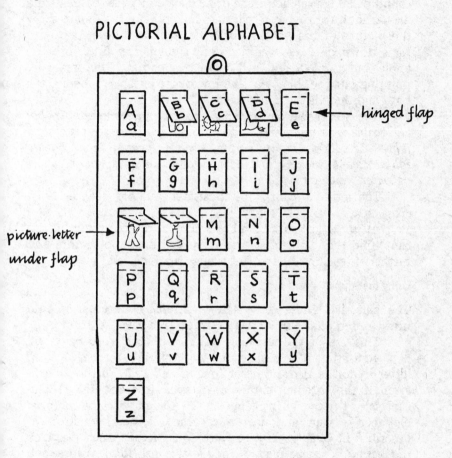

Point out to him that the lower case letter on the flap
looks like an apple, and this can help in finding it. Do not draw
his attention to the upper case letter at this stage.

The next time the story is told, you will see whether your
student can remember what Mary or John found. Leave the

pictures covered and see whether the pupil can find the right picture by looking at the flaps. Help him or her if necessary. Then add the next episode of the story: when Mary or John had found or bought an apple she or he decided to play baseball and had to look for or buy a *bat* and *ball.* Lift up the flap to show the picture of the bat and ball and then, as before, flap both flaps down and see whether your student can find both the apple and the bat and ball. Help him or her if necessary by pointing out the shapes of the lower case letters—"There is the bat *I* and there is the ball close to it, *b.*"

The words we have used for our alphabet are *apple, bat and ball, caterpillar, duck, egg, flower, girl, house, ice-cream, jug, king, light, mouth, nose, orange, peeping pig, queen, rabbit's ears, snake, tree, upside-down umbrella, vase, waves or water, yawn or yell,* and *zip.*

The letter *X* cannot be illustrated but has been left as a cross or kiss.

All these letters should be so familiar to your pupil that he can "find" any object in the story without help, before any further extension of letter-knowledge is attempted.

Using the Alphabet

The pictorial letters with their traditional counterparts could now be used on the word bank dividers (see page 116).

This use of the alphabet letters with the word bank will help your student to realize that not only is *b* the *bat and ball* letter, but it is also the letter for *bus* and *bed.* Further help is given if the listening games are played (see Chapter 7), and especially "I spy." This game can be played with the pictorial alphabet in view and new words can then be introduced as described in Chapter 7. Also, variations of the games described in Chapter 5 can be played using letters instead of pictures and words. In dominoes or bingo or word pairs, the picture and the initial letter can now be matched; and later, they can be matched on the lower- and upper-case letters.

At this stage, the introduction of single letters should be regarded as a *pre-reading* activity. The main activity is still concerned with learning to recognize whole words, and any attempt to analyze these at this stage or to try to get your student to build up words phonically would be a hindrance rather than a help. However, you are laying down a foundation for further progress, and the knowledge of the alphabet gained through this playful introduction will be put to more systematic use in Chapter 7.

It is so important to consolidate one stage before starting the next, that we would like to repeat this word of warning. The introduction of single letters must be treated as a parallel activity to the introduction of whole words at this stage, and no attempt should be made to build words up phonically.

It cannot be assumed that a child always recognizes the difference even between single words and phrases at this stage. Phrases such as "Here y' are" often appear to be treated as single words. The student will not be ready to analyze the structure of words themselves until much later.

However, alphabet blocks and books will help to familiarize your students with letter sounds at this stage also. You can also play at finding letters when out for a walk or when looking at the printed page, such as "See how many bat and ball letters you can find."

Plastic letters that can be bought at any educational toy shop are also useful in familiarizing your pupil with letter shapes. The child will need plenty of practice in sorting these out so that all the *a*s go together, all the *b*s, and so on. When the child can sort out the lower case letters, you can also introduce the upper case letters and practice matching these with the lower case letters.

Letter Names

This pictorial alphabet is introducing your student to the initial sounds made by the different letters in words. As far as reading is concerned, this is the most important aspect of the alphabet.

However, at some stage it is also useful to know the *names* of the letters of the alphabet. This is especially true of the vowel sounds, as in some cases the letter's name and the sound it makes in a word are the same. For instance, in the word age the letter *a* sounds like its name, in the word *ice* the letter *i* sounds like its name, and, similarly with the letters *e, o,* and *u* in the words *eagle, open,* and *ukelele.*

However, we do not suggest that you introduce the letter names until your child is thoroughly familiar with the relationship of the pictorial alphabet to the initial letter sounds of words the child knows. At a much later stage, the letter names will be useful when he is able to use a dictionary.

PICTURE ALPHABET

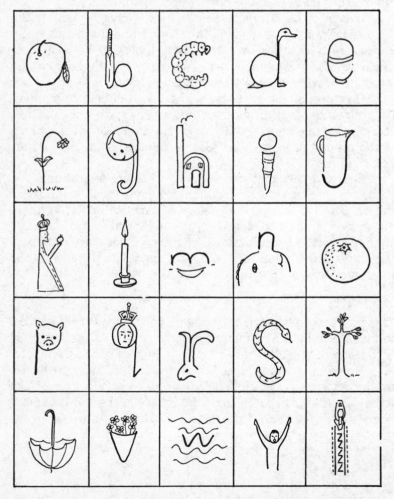

Writing

This introduction to the alphabet is concerned with the visual recognition of letters. We do not suggest that you attempt to teach your child to print letters at this stage. However, this imaginative introduction *will* help the child to appreciate the letter forms pictorially, and the child may attempt to "draw" the *caterpillar* letter (for instance). Do not be in a hurry to capitalize on this but just accept the child's immature version. At a later stage, these early attempts can be shaped into acceptable print.

This pictorial alphabet has been designed so that common confusions between letters such as *b* and *d* and *m* and *w* are largely avoided.

3

Recognizing everyday words

Once your child has a word bank of 20 words, the words in this chapter can be introduced. Much of the activity is related to the home, but at the end of the chapter we suggest adaptation to the classroom.

AT HOME

An ability to recognize labels is a step towards independence and self-help around the house. This can only be achieved with a great deal of perseverance and additional help. The first stage is to include your child in household chores and elicit the child's help systematically. When you are cooking, ask the child to find the *rice*, *sugar*, and *margarine* as you want them. To start with, the child can find them by getting familiar with the shapes and sizes of packages, cans, or jars or by looking inside and getting to know the contents and their names.

Once the child is used to helping you in this way and knows what *flour*, *rice*, and *sugar* look like and what they are called, then the next step is to help him to recognize the labels on cans, jars, and boxes. For this you will need self-adhesive labels to stick on the packages. First, try with only two, and choose two cans that look alike and cannot be distinguished except by looking inside or recognizing the label. Label these, for instance, *rice* and *flour*, and put them side by side on the shelf. Ask him to find the rice for you, and if he gets the wrong one, let him look inside and then look at the label. Do this frequently, and change the position of the cans so that he cannot depend on their placing to get it right.

If he has difficulty, you can accentuate the words to help him. For example, rice can be labeled like this:

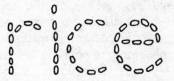

and flour like this:

and you can point to the grains of rice on the rice label and the fine dust of the flour.

At the same time make some cards with SAW words for rice and flour on one side and the TOW words on the other and play games with these. Add the words to the word bank as the child gets to know them. Once he recognizes two labels, introduce a third, and so on. Give the child plenty of practice all the time in helping you in the kitchen so that the child appreciates the value of being able to read the labels when you are busy. Give plenty of encouragement and praise.

Once the child is able to recognize the printed names of several items in the kitchen, vary the procedure and write a list of ingredients you are going to need so that the child can get them ready for you.

You might also make a book, cutting out pictures of household stores with their names printed underneath or with their names in envelopes under each picture. Then see if the child can put the names in the right places.

AN AID TO COMMUNICATION

Some young people have great difficulty in talking, and this can lead to intense frustration and sometimes to temper tantrums when the young person is misunderstood. In some cases, it might be necessary to consider teaching your child one of the alternative forms of communication, such as Paget Gorman sign language, American sign language, or Bliss symbols. You can find out more about these in *Stimulating the Exceptional Child* by Chris Kiernan, Rita Jordan, and Chris Saunders.

However, if your child has begun to recognize words, has some in the word bank, and understands more than he can say, he can use these words to communicate.

BUILDING UP A WORD BANK
FOR COMMUNICATION

Observe your own child carefully and try to fathom the things that he characteristically wants to communicate with you. You will almost certainly already have years of experience interpreting his efforts to communicate behind you and will be able to understand him better than anyone else. However, at times this understanding will fall down, or at times his method of getting the message across will be a crude one. He may drag you to the cupboard if he wants a cookie or throw a tantrum if you give him the wrong one. With care and preparation, you can help to give him a more civilized form of communication.

The suggestions offered here are general and will not necessarily suit your child—you will have to adapt them to his individual needs.

Food and Drink

Food and drink are important to most human beings, both adults and children, and we all develop our own preferences. Temper tantrums at meal times are quite common with handicapped young people who, because of their limited ability to express themselves, have very little choice in the matter. They cannot say that they want more gravy or no peas or that their dinner is too hot or cold. All they can register is their disapproval. Begin by listing your offspring's favorite food or drink. Make cards with the names of the items written on them. You may have to accentuate them on one side of the card and introduce them in games (see Chapter 5).

Once you have built up a few words in this way, put them to use. Keep the cards in a handy box and make sure that they are always available. Let your child practice choosing what he wants to eat or drink by picking out the right word from the bank and showing it to you. At first he has to get the "idea," so start with situations where choice is in order (not necessarily meal times).

Ask the child, "What do you want to eat? A *cookie, ice-cream,* or some *cake*?" Show him the three cards and give him the one he chooses.

Sometimes you can plan ahead and give him a choice at meal time. You can make the choice limited and ask, "What shall we have for lunch—hot dogs and potato chips or hamburgers with french fries?" Put out the cards for these and let him choose the ones he wants.

Do not do this until the child has had plenty of practice with a choice he can eat *immediately*.

Going Out

You may be able to extend the word bank to include words to give him a choice about going out. You have seen in the previous section how you can teach words like *walk, car,* and *bus*. You may have relatives living nearby, and want to include words such as *Grandmother* or *Aunt.* You cannot *always* allow your child to choose, but the danger is that because of his handicap he may *never* be allowed to choose, and this would not only be a mistake but also may make him feel inferior.

Feelings

One of the problems of the handicapped person is that he finds it difficult to convey his feelings. He may be feeling sad or ill or excited but may be unable to express these feelings. This further increases the feeling of isolation.

Make cards that he can use to express feelings. To start with, have a picture on one side of the card and a word on the other. He can then pick out the picture of someone sick in bed when he is feeling sick or a crying face when feeling sad. Then you can teach him the words.

No doubt you will have gotten the idea now and are able to extend these suggestions in ways that are appropriate to your child. You might want to include games to play, other activities, or self-help skills.

Note: Up to now we have used only lower case letters in our reading scheme. However, you will find that many brand names, essential notices, and street signs are printed in capitals.

In most of the rest of this chapter, the examples have been printed in capital letters. Your child may not have too much difficulty in switching to capitals if they are introduced pictorially. Capitals have already been printed on the flaps of the picture alphabet. To familiarize children with them and to help make the link, if extra help is needed, you can play matching games such as Dominoes or Bingo where a capital letter is matched with its lower-case equivalent.

Shopping

We have found that many young people who cannot yet read can recognize patterns of words and designs, if they are sufficiently familiar with them and interested in them. Many of them, for instance, can identify a large number of different favorite records to put on the record player.

The same skill can help them to become gradually more independent or able to assist others. For instance, your child probably goes with you to the stores or to the supermarket. He may merely follow you around, he may inappropriately take things he likes off the shelves, or he may help you to fill your basket. If he is doing this, he will be learning at the same time. This is the first stage of learning—you may have to point to what you want and tell him what it is, but let him put it in your shopping cart or have one of his own. In this way, the goods you buy will become familiar to him and he will also see them around the house and learn to name them and find out their use.

The next stage is to collect some empty bags and wrappers from your purchases. Start with a few and play "store" with them. Ask for the Ajax, Joy, Ivory, and see whether he recognizes them.

Keep a record of the items he knows and the next time you shop, ask him to get them off the shelves one at a time. This time you will not need to point.

Gradually collect more bags, boxes, and cans and introduce these into your game. At the same time, increase the number of articles you ask him to find on the shelves, for example a box of TIDE *and* a tin of AJAX. You will have to choose articles which are near together on the shelves.

MAKING LISTS

Cut out pieces of packages showing the name of the product (only two or three at first) and stick them on to cards.

1. Play store using these cards as your shopping list, and see if your child can find the items on the list.
2. As he collects more items, he can increase the number of items on the list.
3. Use this shopping list in the supermarket and get your child to collect the items on the list from the shelves.
4. Write the name of the product on the back of each card (use the same kind of print as is used on the product). Play store with these—

if your child cannot recognize a word, let him flip the card over to the wrapper or label side.

5. Use these cards in the supermarket.

6. Once your child can recognize the names of products in TOW, make out a proper list for him to help to select goods.

7. If he wants to copy out lists himself, let him do this from the cards. You tell him what goods you want, and he can select the cards.

IMPORTANT WORDS

To get about nowadays, it is important to recognize words that are used on public notices and to be able to act appropriately. These words are usually called a "functional sight vocabulary."

However, it is not enough to be able to recognize these words. They *have* to be introduced in context and linked with the appropriate behavior. Otherwise, although your child may be able to say "stop" when he sees the word STOP, he may still try to cross the road at the wrong time.

The best way to introduce these words is to bide your time and introduce them as they become necessary. For instance, when your child begins to learn about traveling on a bus, you should teach him the words BUS STOP, which he can add to his word-bank.

BUS STOP

These can all be introduced by symbol accentuation as described in the previous section, and on the next page are some more suggestions.

This is a list of some of the words your child will often see on notices in stores and on the street. If he gradually learns to

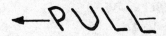

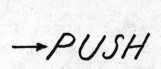

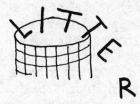

recognize them and *act appropriately*, this will help him to become less dependent on others.

However, we suggest that to learn these words passively at home, is *no* guarantee of appropriate behavior. They should always be linked with the appropriate action, otherwise you may find that a child who can read CLOSED will still knock on the store door.

LIST OF SOME IMPORTANT NOTICES

CLOSED	LADIES
WALK	STOP
OUT	GO
IN	BUS STOP
EXIT	DANGER
WOMEN	KEEP OFF THE GRASS
MEN	ELEVATOR
LITTER	

However, it is far better to make your own list by making a note of the notices in your own neighborhood and deciding which are important. For instance, a child who can recognize a telephone booth may not need to recognize the word TELEPHONE or a child who uses the library would find it helpful if he could identify the different sections.

Following Instructions

Once your child has learned to recognize single words and short phrases on signs, you may want to help him to read instructions on boxes and packages and instructions for making models.

This should not be attempted at this stage, as it requires an infinitely more advanced level of skill. Unfortunately, most instructions on packages are in *very* small type and are often written in very advanced language—sometimes in several foreign languages. For instance, the instructions on a bottle of Clorox read "Caution—Clorox may be harmful if swallowed or may cause severe eye irritation if splashed in eyes. Call physician. Not to be taken internally. Keep away from children." That is a comparatively simple set of instructions. At this stage, you will simply have to tell your child the important things about the products he uses.

In Chapter 4 you will find more suggestions that will gradually help him towards greater independence.

ADAPTATION TO SCHOOL

This chapter has been about experiences in and around the home.

Schools will often have activities that correspond and lend themselves to similar use. For instance, they may have a "store"; they take their pupils shopping in supermarkets; they have school meals and school outings; they help their older pupils to learn to catch buses and use the telephone.

The appropriate vocabulary can be linked with all these activities; and again, this is an opportunity for cooperation between school and home.

4

The language–experience approach: making your own books

INTRODUCTION

The first words the child will recognize will be those that are intimately connected with his own life and that he sees very often. For instance, many children can recognize their own name long before they recognize any other words. Other young people learn to recognize words that are very important to them because they reflect their own interests. One sixteen-year-old boy who could not read one word on an early word list was passionately interested in football and could read the words Dallas Cowboys, New York Jets and the names of most of the other major football teams without any difficulty. Similarly, a teenage girl who was interested in cooking was able to pick out the names of ingredients from recipe books.

This showed that both of these young people were ready to read more, if given the appropriate opportunity. However, they were not yet ready for early "readers," because not only is it difficult to find readers that reflect a teenager's interests and motivate him to learn, but also such readers often use unfamiliar words and turns of phrase.

For such young people, an individual approach will be described in this chapter. This will be done in such a way that the young person will acquire the skills needed for reading printed books and eventually an unfamiliar text. This approach is now frequently used in schools and is called the *Language-Experience* approach to the teaching of reading.

It has the added advantage of ensuring that the pupils always understand what they are reading. It is meaningful to them and they are not simply "word calling."

However, not all children will be ready for this approach. How do we know that our child is ready?

If you have already been working on symbol accentuation and your child has built up a word bank of twenty to thirty words, he will probably be ready to begin learning through language-experience. Alternatively, if he is interested in books, can recognize pictures, and can pick out records by looking at the covers, and has learned to recognize a few words on his own, such as his own name and perhaps the words on familiar boxes—Ivory or cornflakes—it is worth trying this method. In case of difficulty, go back to symbol accentuation.

WHAT IS THE LANGUAGE-EXPERIENCE APPROACH?

You cannot use commercially produced reading matter for this approach, because all the reading material arises from the child's own experience and *is in his own words*. This ensures not only that he knows what he is reading about but also that it is meaningful to him and reflects his own interests. It also means that he is not trying to reproduce unfamiliar stilted language but is learning that the written word is speech written down.

Basically, what you will be doing is using your child's own interests and pictures he has chosen to make a series of scrap books or picture books with a caption under each picture. If each book is short, with no more than six pictures, he will feel less insecure and will have the satisfaction of building up a library of his own.

WHAT TOPICS WILL BE SUITABLE FOR THESE BOOKS?

The answer to this question is *virtually anything that interests your child.* You may have to choose the subject of the first book, but after that your child will probably suggest ideas. Subjects can be as varied as favorite foods, rock stars, football players, fashions, visits to the stores, baseball, or pets.

Some children are characteristically apathetic, and, in this case, you may have to stage riveting experiences before making a book about them. You may have to do this anyway when introducing a new topic. The element of surprise and anticipation is important here, but no elaborate preparation is needed. For instance, you could wrap a few objects up in a shoe box and get your child to find them, talk about them, and use them as the subject of a book. You may decide to take him on a special trip. If so, build up his anticipation beforehand, and he is then likely to get the most out of this experience and be ready to talk about it afterwards. More practical suggestions will be included in this chapter.

HOW TO BEGIN

Before you begin, you will probably have to suggest the topic of the first book, but involve your child as much as possible and always be prepared to follow suggestions. If you are at a loss to think of a topic, the first book can be about the child or the family. If he can draw, he could draw himself for the first illustration, and, perhaps, the other pictures could be on the topic of body parts or his clothes. If he does not want to draw, you could choose illustrations from mail order catalogues, magazines, or family photographs. However, you do not need to use pictures for these books. It often adds to the interest if the young person collects things from his own expeditions or experiences. For instance, he could collect leaves from trees which could be pressed and glued to pages. Some young people like collecting bus tickets or stamps.

MAKING THE BOOKS

Materials

Paper: drawing paper, brown paper, typing paper, or wallpaper for the pages.

Cardboard: any plain cardboard will do—postcards, sheets of thin cardboard, or stiff paper for making the captions.

Other: felt tip pens, scissors, glue, staples of needle and thread, and used envelopes.

Pictures, or crayons for drawing illustrations.

Method

Prepare a few books, either by making them yourself or using drawing books or note books. Notebooks purchased at the dime store will have too many pages. Two folded pages are enough for a reading booklet. Scrap books are also suitable and can be divided into several booklets.

If you are making your own booklets, here are a few suggestions: Fold over two sheets of paper; staple down the middle or sew as follows:

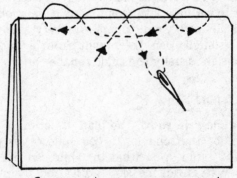

Sewing the back of the book

Paste a used envelope on to the bottom of each page:

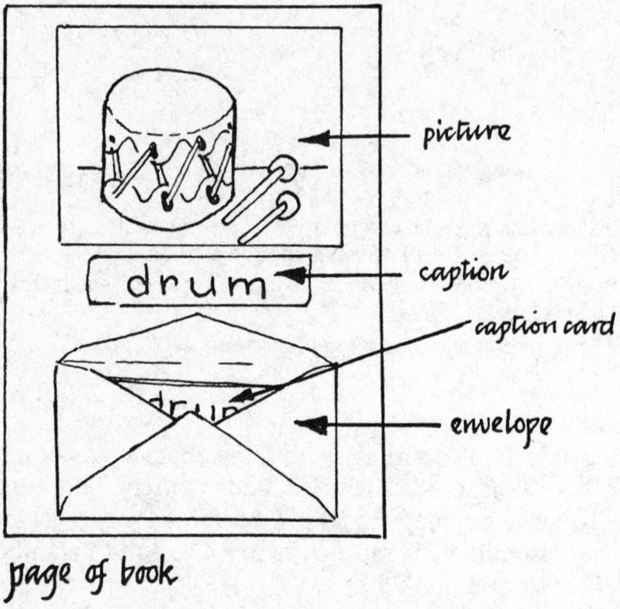

picture

caption

caption card

envelope

page of book

Paste a caption under the picture and make a separate word-card to put into the envelope. The word-card strips should be at least one inch by three inches in dimension. Words should be printed in lower case letters and should be about a third of an inch high. If you want to make a very professional job of the book, stencils can be bought from a good art shop. Typed captions are usually too small for the early books.

PLAN OF ACTION

The following diagram shows the plan of action to be followed at every stage of the scheme. If you follow this plan, it will ensure that you build upon what the child can already do, that you increase his confidence and motivation by play at every stage. and that new knowledge is added on a sure foundation.

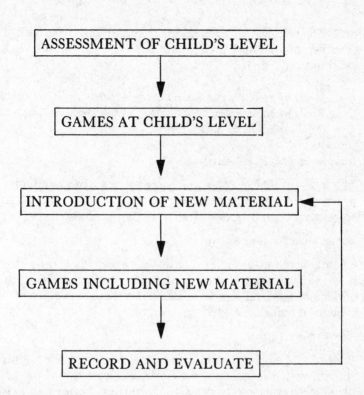

```
┌─────────────────────────────────┐
│   ASSESSMENT OF CHILD'S LEVEL   │
└─────────────────────────────────┘
                 │
                 ▼
┌─────────────────────────────┐
│   GAMES AT CHILD'S LEVEL    │
└─────────────────────────────┘
                 │
                 ▼
┌───────────────────────────────────┐
│   INTRODUCTION OF NEW MATERIAL    │◄────┐
└───────────────────────────────────┘     │
                 │                         │
                 ▼                         │
┌───────────────────────────────────┐     │
│   GAMES INCLUDING NEW MATERIAL    │     │
└───────────────────────────────────┘     │
                 │                         │
                 ▼                         │
┌───────────────────────────────┐         │
│   RECORD AND EVALUATE         │─────────┘
└───────────────────────────────┘
```

Assessment of Child's Level

The checklists at the beginning of the book will help you to assess the level of your child's ability—what he can already do. This is your starting point (recognize pictures, recognize his own name, read road signs, read a simple sentence).

Games at Child's Level

No new material should be introduced at this point. If he can only recognize pictures, the games should be played with familiar pictures; if he can recognize a few words, games should be played with the words he knows. This will not only consolidate his knowledge, but will also provide an introduction to the rules of a variety of games that will be played later with new material.

The choice of games will depend upon individual preference, but should include one from each of the following headings:

> *Matching games:* dominoes, bingo, word pairs
> *Recognition games:* word spotting, find the word (see Chapter 5)
> *Games to aid recall:* pick a card

Introduction of New Material

The rest of this chapter will suggest ways of introducing new material such as words and sentences. However, it is important to remember to introduce only one new skill at a time.

Games Including New Material

At this stage you should continue to play the games that you have already taught your child. The new material should be added to the well known material so that your child is always certain of some success.

Record and Evaluate

Recording progress can be carried out at two levels: an informal record, which is essential for both the parents and the child to be able to see the progress that is being made, and a formal record for teachers.

An informal record is easy to keep—as soon as your child has learned a new word properly—he can pick it out from a display of other words when you name it and can name it himself confidently on three separate occasions without help from you—you should put a card with the word printed on it into the word bank. The word bank is simply a box divided up alphabetically with word cards in it. If you pencil in the date on which you added the card to the bank, you will have a handy record of progress. The keeping of formal records will be explained in Chapter 9.

Evaluation is merely taking stock of the situation. If your child is having difficulty, you may have to backtrack and consolidate an earlier stage. If he is progressing rapidly, you may have to increase your rate of introduction of new material.

The preceding plan of action can ideally lead to closer collaboration between home and school, where each plays the part for which he is best fitted. Although parents are sometimes in a position to follow the entire plan, many are not and feel that teaching should be carried out by the professionals. However, teachers in school don't have the time to give all the students the individual attention they may need as often as they would like and the practice and generalization of skills which is required.

An ideal plan would be for the assessment to be carried out at school, as well as the teaching of new material and keeping of formal records. The practice games would then be played at home. Many parents of handicapped children have commented on their children's few interests and their inability to occupy their spare time.

We have found that these parents appreciate having teaching games sent home; the young people themselves like to feel that they, like their siblings, have homework to do.

We have also found that the less able child is often the solitary child and that his occupations are also solitary. The advantage of teaching games may be that they help the child to cooperate and take turns in more sociable activities that involve not only parents but also grandparents, siblings, and neighboring friends.

In our experience, fathers are often not sufficiently involved with handicapped children. Yet they are often excellent teachers and can also design new games to play.

PUTTING THE PLAN INTO ACTION

Now you are ready to begin. To make it easy to follow, we will describe the plan in stages. How quickly you can go through each stage and on to the next will depend upon the individual child. For some chidren you will need to make several books at stage one before moving on to stage two, and with others you may need only one or two books at this level.

It is important to get off to a good start and let your child experience achievement right from the beginning. This means choosing your first topic carefully. Your first word must be one your child already uses, as this will give him confidence. For instance, you could start by using his own name.

Page one.   Let your child draw a picture for the top of the first page, or help choose a picture and cut it out of a catalogue or magazine and glue it to the page. Share the interest in this activity with your child, talk about the picture, and then ask him what to call it. At this stage, print the word he suggests under the picture and on a separate card to be kept in the envelope. Let him watch you printing the two words so that he can see that they match.

Activities.   Although you have only one picture and one word, you can already start an activity that will help recognition practice. Take two or three blank word cards and print words on them in the same type as the target word. Choose words with about the same number of letters as the target word but ones not starting with the same letter. Leave the book open at the first page, with the caption showing under the picture. Ask the child to close his eyes as you spread three or four word cards out on the table, including the target word. Ask your child if he can find the *cat* card (target card) and put it back in its envelope. He may be able to pick it out straight away or he may need to check by matching it with the caption in the book. He will learn most if he does the checking himself, so resist the temptation of "helping" him too much by saying "that's right" or "wrong." Encourage him to find out whether it is right or wrong.

Depending on your child's success with this activity, make it simpler or more difficult. To make it easier, use fewer cards for him to scan and put them nearer together. Start, for instance, with a choice of two cards that look very different, and, only after he can pick out the target word confidently, introduce a third card. To make it more difficult, use more cards so that the search takes longer, and choose words that look similar. Spread the cards out so that your child must really look carefully at them all and learn to search. Then try covering up the caption in the book and see whether he can still pick out his target card. Once he has picked it out, he can still check himself by uncovering the caption in the book and seeing whether it matches; or you can print a number of duplicate target cards and a few more distractors (other words). Spread these out on the table or floor and have a game to see who can find the most *cats* first.

Page two.   Another picture on your favorite topic is chosen for page two, and again your child suggests a name for it.

Activities.   Now that your child has two word cards and two pictures, he can help to put the cards back into the right envelopes at the end of each session, checking by matching them with the caption word himself and later seeing if he can sort them even when the caption word is covered up.

Page three to the end of the book.   Continue to add pictures and words on each page and play sorting games with the new words until all the pages (four to six) have been completed. Now list all the words on the back cover and see if your child can read these. If he cannot, go back to playing with the separate word cards. Suggestions for games will be found in the games chapter, but you could play a simple race game at this stage with a dice. Mark out a route on a large piece of cardboard and use two little toys or chips. Place the word cards face down in a pile. Each player then throws the dice, moves the appropriate number of spaces forward, and then takes a card from the top of the pile. If he can read it, he either has an extra throw or takes two extra steps forward. If your child has difficulty in using conventional dice, make a simpler one with only one, two, or three spots on the sides.

You will probably need to make several booklets on different topics at stage one before moving on to stage two. Be sure that your child has sufficient practice in recognizing and reading the words in each book before starting a new one. As soon as a child can read a word and pick it out from a display without help, this word can be added to his word bank (see Chapter 9).

Stage Two: Putting Words Together

As you make the books at stage one with single words, you will find your child is usually using more than one word to describe each picture. He may be suggesting that you write *black cat*, or *my crayons*, or *Daddy fishing*. However, his ability to read will not be as advanced as his ability to speak, and, for this reason, the first books should be the single-word level. Once he has mastered these, you can start putting more than one word on each page. Start with two words and select these from his description. Rememeber to *use his own words* and do not be tempted to improve on them at this stage. For instance, you may have phrases such as: *black dog, my nose, more books, Mommy sleeping, Johnny sad*, and so on. Now for each page you will have a caption and *two* cards in the envelope. He will now have to put the cards in the *right order* as well as finding the correct cards for each page. Let him use the captions as a means of checking himself, and then try to sort out the cards with the captions covered. Participate in this activity and see if he can spot your deliberate mistakes—*dog black* instead of *black dog*—then let him correct you.

As before, make a list of all the words in the book on the back page when the book is finished, and see whether he can read these without the help of the pictures. If he cannot, play more games with the separate word cards. If he can, you can go on to playing this game:

New phrases. Make duplicate cards for all the words in the book. Each player has a set of cards and makes new phrases with them. For instance, if the phrases *black dog, my nose, more books, Mommy sleeping, John dancing*, and *lovely dinner* had been chosen for the book, then many new phrases can be made with these words, such as *my dog, my dinner, more dinner, black nose, John black, dog sleeping*.

Do not be afraid of humor. If some of these phrases are rather absurd, they will be even more likely to be remembered.

Three words. When your child can competently cope with two-word captions, you can introduce a new book with three-word captions. Some of these will turn out as complete sentences, such as *baby has more, John eats cereal, black dog sleeps*, and so on. However, do not insist on fully formed sentences; accept phrases as well, such as *pretty blue mug, cup on shelf*, and so on. Again remember to use your child's own words. If you change them, he will probably read them incorrectly, forgetting your version, and substituting his own. As before, make sure that your child cannot only recognize the whole phrase when he sees it, but that he can also put each phrase back in the right order when they get "mixed up," and recognize each single word in the phrase. When he can do this, you can show him how to make many new phrases and sentences himself. For instance, from *John eats cereal*, you can introduce all the other things John likes to eat and make new sentences: *John eats meat*, John *eats Twinkies, and so on.*

Stage Three: Complete Sentences

At this stage you will use your child's complete sentences for your captions, e.g. *Daddy's putting the car away. This is me at the beach. A car is passing a truck.*

By using complete sentences, your child will begin to read words such as *the, and*, *this*, *here*, *on*, *at*, and *over*, which do not make sense on their own but only in the context of a sentence, yet it is important to be able to read these words, as they will occur again and again in reading books.

As before, all the words in the reading book should be listed at the back of the book and also collected in the word bank. These words can be combined to make new sentences. As before, your child will need lots of practice, and many games (listed in Chapter 5) can be played with these new words. At this stage, it is best to make two sets of word cards. The first set should be the whole sentence. For the second set, you first print the whole sentence on one card and then show your child how to cut it up into single words, sort them, and put them together again in the right order.

However, apart from being able to play sorting games and Bingo with the words in the text, your child's main achievement at this stage will be his reading book, which he can read to himself, to you, or to other children. This is very rewarding, especially because many handicapped children have seen others read and yet have not been able to do it themselves. At this stage, if the books are short ones, you will gradually be building up a library of individual books your child can read.

WIDENING EXPERIENCE

In this method, new experiences, making books about them, and reading the books to refresh your memory of those experiences go hand in hand. If your child's experience is extremely limited, he will only be able to suggest the text on a limited number of subjects. After a time he may dry up and the books will become boring and repetitive. Now is the time to deliberately set about widening his experience and to give him new ideas and skills out of which new reading matter will arise. Here are a few suggestions:

Myself

A book could be made of body parts, but a very young child or a very handicapped person may neither know the names of all the body parts or know where they are. If he does not, now is the time to give him this new experience. The obvious way to do this is to take a tip from mothers with babies and play a finding game: find your nose, eyes, fingers, and elbow. Now find my nose and my eyes. This can also be played with dolls and soft toys. With an older child you can either make or buy a cut-out cardboard figure that is made like a jigsaw puzzle and has to be reassembled. (You can buy such cut-outs at good toy shops, and suppliers will be listed at the back of this book). The natural language you will use to help your child to do this will help to teach him the correct names for the different parts of the body. Another active game for learning the body parts and where they are is "Simon Says." The leader calls out "Simon says touch your hair" or "touch your toes," etc. The one to follow instructions first is the winner. Play the games first and *then* make the book, not the other way round.

My Favorite Foods

This book usually needs less preparation than most. However, it is important to ensure that your child has some say in the choice of what he eats, and, if possible, in the preparation of food. The more actively involved he is in helping to roll out pastry, put the potatoes in the bowl, or, later, to make a cup of tea and butter the bread, the more likely he is to remember the appropriate words to describe what he eats.

My Clothes, My Friends, My Toys, My Interests

Young people are usually interested in whatever their parents are doing. Children who have had the opportunity to watch their father wash the car, change a tire, or put water into the radiator, and, especially those children who have been allowed to help, often have a surprising knowledge of the names of parts of the engine. Similarly, children who have been allowed to watch meals being prepared and have been given the opportunity to help according to their capacity will know far more about cooking than those who have not.

Here are some suggestions for books that might arise out of helping an adult:

Cars and car engines, gardening tools and plants, cooking meals, decorating the house, spring cleaning, changing a fuse, or washing the clothes.

Everyday Events

We have found that many teenage handicapped boys and girls are taken by their parents everywhere. They go with them shopping, to a restaurant, on a trip, camping, and so on. However, not all of them benefit as much as they might by these experiences. Some seem apathetic, perhaps because they have not had much choice about these activities and have had to fit in with the family arrangements. Their part in the whole event has been a passive one. Parents who have made sure that their child has an active role to play in these events have noted a different attitude. One parent who started to let her child find goods for her on the shelves when she went to the supermarket was astonished by the child's change in attitude to shopping, and the new interest also had the added benefit of making the child more independent.

Another reason that children do not always benefit from these everyday events is that they have not been sufficiently prepared beforehand.

Here is where individual books are very useful.

A few years ago we carried out an experiment with a group of willing parents to illustrate the beneficial effects of preparation, active participation and individual scrap books. A group of mentally handicapped children and a group of younger normal children, all of whom were fortunate in having concerned parents who took them shopping, to the park, and on trips were compared in order to see how much each had benefited from these experiences, and how much they knew about the immediate neighborhood. It was a simple test that the young people enjoyed. They had to arrange the contents of a number of bags, each containing five model objects. One of these objects would be connected with each topic and the others would be distractors. For instance, if the subject of one bag was the fire station, one object would be a miniature fireman. The young people talked about their visit to the fire station and arranged the objects in whatever way they wished, named them, and were then asked to pick out the one that they would find at the fire station. The results were that the much younger normal children were more often correct in picking out the right object than the older handicapped children, although the older children had more experience behind them.

With the full cooperation of the parents, it was then decided to carry out another experiment. The handicapped children were randomly divided into two groups. All the parents were visited regularly to talk about their child's progress. However, one group of parents were given very general suggestions for work with their children, while the other group undertook to carry out a specific program. We called this program *yesterday, today, and tomorrow*. Whenever they knew that a certain event was going to take place, such as a visit to the hairdressers, or to the post office, they would prepare their child the day before by telling him exactly what was going to happen. They also agreed to talk about the event when it was taking place and, when they came home, to stick a reminder of the event into a scrap book, which would be a talking point in the days to come. The reminder could be a picture or a receipt or anything else appropriate. At the end of the experiment, the two groups of children were again asked to select items from the experience bags. The group whose parents had made the scrap books were much better at picking out the appropriate objects than the other group.

Adaptation for School and Classroom

Most special schools organize trips and treats for their pupils. These are sometimes day trips, vacations such as camping trips. They can be prepared for in the same way as we have suggested here. Provide subjects for each student's individual book. Even lesser activities, like someone's birthday in school or going shopping or making candy, can become a book. It is important to make books for each individual and make them different from each other.

In the case of the experiment described above, no captions were written in the scrap book; but if these were included, the individual books would be even more effective, because the children could read them whenever they wished. With such preparation, books could be made from many day-to-day events: going to the supermarket, mailing a letter, or going to the hairdressers.

Outings and Treats

In our experiment, the parents also prepared the children as before and made scrapbooks on the subject of special treats. If captions are put under the pictures, these will be good subjects for individual reading books.

Subjects could include: a visit to the zoo, a visit to the

circus, a wedding, a school concert, a birthday party, or a trip to a city.

Story Books

There are many inexpensive story books on the market with interesting pictures, though the text itself is often far too difficult for your child to read. A good idea is to cover up the text of one of these with plain white paper and let your child look at the pictures and tell his own story. You can then print his version on the blank page and let him read it back to you. If you have been in the habit of telling your child stories and also reading to him (see Chapter 6), he will be much more able to make up his own. He may use phrases he has heard you use, such as "Once upon a time . . . ," but the advantage will be that he will also be able to read them and may later on recognize these phrases in other books.

Information Books

We have found that many handicapped teenagers who may not be able to read at all have quite sophisticated interests. One boy, for instance, was always interested in anything electrical. His father, wisely, encouraged this interest, but, foreseeing the danger of letting his son play with electrical equipment without knowing the proper procedure, taught him how to change a fuse and change a light bulb. This boy liked looking at the pictures in books on electricity, but the text meant nothing to him. However, he did know something about each picture or diagram. A beginners' book on electricity would provide him with his own reading book. The text could be covered up and his own version substituted.

Another teenager, again a non-reader, had helped his father in a practical way in cleaning, painting, and repairing cars. As a result, he was not only knowledgeable about different makes of cars but also about engine parts. A girl was very interested in cooking and was able to prepare several simple dishes. Another young man was an accomplished accordion player. They attended special education schools, and none of them could read or write. For these teenagers with sophisticated interests, it is possible to buy well illustrated information books. In each case, if the text is covered with a sheet of plain white paper, the young person can discuss the pictures in turn and a new text can be printed at his own level of understanding.

Hobbies

If your child already has several hobbies, there will be no problems, and you can collect pictures and material related to these. Here are a few suggestions: knitting, sewing, stamps, swimming, horse riding, indoor plants, bird watching, cooking, gardening, painting, model making, or photography.

Unfortunately many handicapped children and young people have no hobbies or special interests to talk about. In this case, the interest has to be fostered first and has to become a familiar experience before a book is attempted.

Humor

Many handicapped people respond to humor and appreciate the absurd situation.

Remember these are *their* books. Accept jokes and humorous situations at their own level. There are many ways of approaching this. One backward reader that we knew, learned to begin to read by making his own "joke" book. He used the limited number of words that he could recognize and created simple sentences from them by putting the cards in order. Then he added illustrations.

The book ran something like this: *I am a dog. No I am not a dog. I am a boy. I am a potato. No I am not a potato. I am a boy.*

This was not very sophisticated humor, and had it been the teacher who had produced the book, it might have been rather patronizing. However, because the boy had produced it himself, he found it hilarious, especially when he went on in the same vein using his teacher's name in place of his own. And making this book *was* teaching that boy a great deal. The repetition helped in his recognition of words, it was an introduction to books, and it taught him about word order and the construction of sentences.

Most children also like comic books, even if adults do not consider them very uplifting. Your child will probably look at the pictures in them and have his own favorite characters before he is able to read the text. Why not cut out some of these illustrations and let him tell you about them: Garfield is fat and lazy. Then write his words under the picture.

At the next level, some children will have learned a few riddles and might enjoy making a riddle book.

At the next level, some children will have learned a few riddles and might enjoy making a riddle book.

Yet others may enjoy "elephant" jokes along the lines of, "How many elephants can you get in the back seat of a car?"

Most children can enjoy books of simple visual jokes of the slipping-on-banana-peel kind. These can be favorite reading matter whether home-drawn or cut out of magazines and newspapers.

Poetry and Rhymes

If your child can already recite a poem or a rhyme (a nursery rhyme for instance), make this into a book.

If his repertoire is very limited, teach him some more (action rhymes are particularly suitable).

Literature

In the chapter on story telling, we have suggested how you can help your child to appreciate stories and literature by reading to him and telling him stories. Remember that before man learned to read and write, much of the folk lore and literature was handed down by word of mouth. These folk tales are still favorites with children, and many of them encompass a great deal of repetition, such as The Gingerbread Man. After repeated telling, children tend to learn these stories "by heart." So instead of telling them the story, see if they can begin to tell it to you. They may or may not use the exact words of the original, but it does not matter. Now is the time to make books of stories retold in their own words.

How to Do It Series

You will often find yourself trying to teach your child a new skill, such as how to make a paper airplane, a Christmas card, a model car, or a kite. Anyone who has tried to do this with a handicapped child will know that careful preparation is necessary to avoid frustration. You have to analyze each stage of the task (task analysis), and break it down into small steps. Now, once the child has mastered each step, you can make a How to Do It book together. Illustrate each page, and keep the instructions simple, such as, "fold the paper," "put a dab of glue on each corner," and so on. He may later find these books useful for reference when he wants to remind himself about how to make something.

The Media

We have found in our research that the leisure time activities and interests of many handicapped young people are very limited. However, almost invariably they watch television and listen to the radio or to records. Many teenagers we visited could tell us more about their favorite television programs, records, and movie stars than about anything else. These can be used as the subject of their books, and suitable illustrations are readily available in *People Magazine*, *TV Guide*, and in the newspapers.

Creating New Experiences

You may have to create new experiences to arouse your child's interest and give him something to talk about. At the one-word level and beyond, this can be simply done by wrapping up a series of objects and putting them into a box for the child to find. Build up the anticipation and involvement by making him guess what is in each package before he is allowed to open it. You may find that this guessing is the most interesting part of the conversation, in which case jot down what the child says and use it as your text, such as "I think it's a spoon." Of course, some children will only be able to guess once they have unwrapped the object, and then your text may consist of a single label word.

Another way to arouse interest is to produce an unfamiliar object at the beginning of each session. Do not tell the child what it is or what it is used for but let him guess. Jot down what he says and use this as your text to print in the book.

Another way to arouse interest is a more complex guessing game. You mime an action and get the child to guess what you are doing or who you are. His guesses can be the text for an action book. Let him also take a turn in miming, and tell you what he is doing only after you have guessed (this is similar to "charades.")

READING AND WRITING

You will probably have noted that we have not mentioned writing in this book, and you may feel that reading and writing should go together as they are obviously related to one another.

We have done this deliberately, as this is primarily a book about learning to read. The skills required in learning to write are by no means the same as those required in learning to read although some of them overlap. A child taught by our methods can learn to read even though he cannot be taught to write.

However, if you use the language-experience approach, you will find that your child may want to "do it himself" when he has seen you writing the captions repeatedly. At first he may take part by "pretending" to write captions for himself in indecipherable scribble.

If he becomes dissatisfied with this and shows he is eager and ready to learn to write, then he should be encouraged. There are several ways of encouraging him. One is to let him trace the letters of a word. You may have to start by printing the word larger than usual and even guiding his hand. Guiding his hand is quite important at this stage, for, if a child learns to form letters the wrong way, this will lead to difficulties later on.

Many children, once you have written a caption, like to copy it underneath and should be allowed to do so. Again make sure each letter is correctly formed.

Many educational suppliers make plastic stencils that a child can use, and these are especially designed to ensure correct letter formation. You could also use these stencils when making the books.

However, in our experience, there are children able to acquire a sight vocabulary before they have acquired the basic control necessary for writing. You can easily check this. Letters of the alphabet are all formed from a combination of straight and curved lines that have to be accurately copied. See whether your child can copy a circle, a square (without rounded corners), a cross, a triangle, an arch, and an "S" shape. If he can do all these accurately and holds his pencil correctly, he will probably be able to help by copying or tracing the captions. If not, he will need to practice writing patterns. These should be done on large sheets of paper with a large crayon or paint brush at first. You can find out about writing patterns in any handwriting book for infant schools.

Once your child has had plenty of practice in copying words and letters, you could try him with a familiar short word without a copy. Remember that this requires quite a high level of skill, as anyone trying to learn the Greek alphabet will appreciate.

To repeat, reading and writing require different skills which should be taught separately. Unless writing comes easily to your child, it is best to follow this reading scheme in the way outlined—*you* do all the writing and printing, but the child uses your cards to learn from in many different ways, including reordering them to make new sentences.

If you want to teach him to write, do this as a separate activity.

5

Games to play

INTRODUCTION

Although this chapter is particularly directed to parents, we
suggest that, ideally teachers should introduce the initial teaching of new words and parents should consolidate this teaching
by means of games played at home. However, games are also
important at school, and often two or more children are playing together and make good use of the time when they are not
having individual instruction.

Whether played at home or in school, these reading games
are of vital importance in the teaching of reading to the mentally handicapped.

WHY GAMES

Overlearning

It is generally agreed that mentally handicapped children need
a great deal of repetition at each stage before they can master
a new skill and make it their own. Once they have done this,

they are not likely to forget. In the past, this "overlearning," or practice of new skills, was sometimes achieved by means of drill. In order to make this drill more palatable, reinforcers or rewards were used. Each time the child gave a correct answer, he was praised or perhaps given a sweet or token that he could later exchange for something he wanted. With some children, these extrinsic rewards may be necessary to begin with in order to get them going. However, if the learning is turned into a game, these rewards usually become unnecessary. Playing the game becomes reward in itself. Throughout history, people have practiced their skills through playing games. Chess is one example, and more recently, Scrabble.

Social Aspects

Part of growing up is concerned with learning to do things with other people, to take turns, to talk to others, to learn to lose gracefully, as well as to win. Some handicapped children do not get enough opportunity to learn the social aspects of living and become isolated. By playing a game with another person, a child begins to learn these lessons.

Normalization

In recreation, a handicapped person can compete on equal terms with anyone else, so long as he knows how to play the game. This is often not true of other activities in which lack of skill may be all too apparent. Games of chance are particularly good in this respect, as winning or losing is not dependent upon skill.

We have found that normal brothers and sisters and neighbors' children will often enjoy a simple game of chance and will happily join in with their less able companion.

Independent Choice

There are so many things a handicapped person has to be taught, that it is easy to lose sight of his need to choose his own occupation and, at times, to be the "teacher" instead of always the student. If you are careful to introduce a variety of games at the right level and make sure that you fade out your own role as director of the game, the handicapped person has the opportunity to choose his own game, to show others how to play it, and to make his own variations.

GUIDELINES

One Thing at a Time

It is easy to make the mistake of trying to introduce more than one new thing at a time. We forget that the rules for playing a very simple game may be new for our child—for instance, matching cards, taking turns, throwing a dice. It is best to introduce each game in its simplest version, so that the player can concentrate on learning the rules. Then gradually introduce more complex material into the same game, so that the player is mastering one thing at a time. Remember that the game should be played for its own sake and for the enjoyment the child gets out of it, so be wary of making it too difficult. Your child will still be learning if he repeats an easy game over and over again.

Learning New Skills

Many different skills are involved in learning to read, and we have divided the games into categories to indicate which skills are involved.

Matching. The first category is matching—matching two pictures or words which are identical—and then matching a picture with a symbol accentuated word or with a word in traditional orthography, or matching a word written in its accentuated form with one written in traditional orthography.

Recognition. The second category is concerned with recognition—being able to pick out a named picture from a number of others, an accentuated word, or a word written in traditional orthography. Simple versions of these games should be played at first, with only a very few examples to choose from. In some cases, you may have to start with only two examples, with the child having to pick out the one you name. You can then make it harder by adding more examples one at a time. Some children find these games quite difficult because they have not learned to scan, to look at every picture or word before making up their minds which one to pick. We can appreciate the difficulty of introducing too many examples, because we ourselves find it easy to recognize our friends at home but quite difficult to pick them out in a crowd.

Also, we have to remember that the more unlike the examples are, the easier it is to pick out the right one. For instance, it is difficult to pick out the word, *cat*, from other words that look alike, such as *mat*, *cap*, *cot*, *can*, *cup*, and *hat*, whereas it is far easier to pick out *cat* from a display of very dissimilar words such as *refrigerator*, *mouse*, *caterpillar*, and *frog*.

Start by making the game easy and gradually make it more difficult, so that the child is making finer discriminations. If necessary, the first round of the game can be made very easy, with the key word written and the other words in picture form.

Recall. The skill that we most often associate with reading is that of recall—being able to look at a written word and say it or read it. This can be a difficult skill to learn at first because, unlike the skill of recognition, we now have an unlimited choice of which words it might be.

For this reason, we give the child extra clues at first to help recall, such as "This is an animal, what is it?"

Nor does recall necessarily become easier as the pupil learns to recognize more words. In some ways, it becomes more difficult. At first he may have recognized the word *cat* because it began with *c* or because it is the only short word he has learned. Later he may confuse the word with other short words beginning with *c* and looking very similar, such as *cot*. Take this into account if your student seems to be regressing.

Self-Checking

It is important to organize the games you play so that your student can become increasingly independent of his teacher. If the game has been well chosen, you will not need to be continually prompting your student, when he falters or makes a mistake. For this reason, we use self-checking devices in the games we have suggested. If he cannot read a word, he can turn the card over and see the symbol accentuated word (SAW) or the picture on the other side. We have found that this encourages the student to make the maximum effort. Confident that there is a way out if things become too difficult, he may be more willing to make the effort to try to do without it.

Winning and Losing

However handicapped a child is, it is important to respect him as a person. This entails letting him lose as well as win. This requires rather careful adjustment. We have found that in order to enjoy a game, a child needs to win very frequently at the beginning. Once the game is familiar and he likes playing it, he will not be put off by losing and this, in fact, may whet his appetite for more. Games of chance are very good in this respect, as nobody has had to engineer the game so that one person wins. Learning to lose is as important as enjoying winning. Once a child has learned to play a game, another child may prove a better opponent than an adult. Children are usually very strict about fair play and teach each other a lot.

Variety and Choice

In order to make sure the child doesn't get bored, it is important to introduce a variety of games. It is then possible for your student to exercise his right to choose a game to play. We have also found that, once the student becomes familiar with a game, he will start to introduce his own variations, which should be encouraged. It is also important to change roles with your pupil so that you are not always the initiator or leader of the game.

Levels of Difficulty

Most of the games described here are relatively easy to learn and do not include complicated rules or procedures. Once the basic game has been learned, the content can be altered to include increasingly difficult material. This has the advantage that the game is familiar but not boring, because new challenges are introduced step by step. These games will be described as "Games with simple rules."

Some games will be included which are more difficult,

because they do not depend only upon your student's ability to recognize words but require other pre-requisite skills. For instance, in order to play a race game, the child will need to be able to recognize a number of dots on a dice, to be able to move a counter in the right direction for the appropriate number of steps, and, of course, to be ready to take turns. These will be described as "More difficult games."

GAMES WITH SIMPLE RULES

Matching Games:
Identical Matching

Word Pairs.   A game played like Concentration requiring two cards of each word in the word bank. These are spread face down on the table. The player turns two cards over without changing their position on the table and reads them. The game is to collect identical pairs. If the two cards turned up are not the same, they are turned face down again. If a player turns up a pair, he keeps these and has another turn. The player with the most pairs wins.

Bingo.   Each player has a card marked out into squares. On each square is a word or picture from the word or picture bank. The dealer picks up and shows each card from the bank in turn. If it corresponds with a square on a player's card, he claims it. The player with the entire card covered up first is the winner.

Dominoes.   Played like ordinary dominoes, but with pictures or words on the dominoes instead of spots.

Find the partner.   Two sets of identical cards are prepared (pictures or words). One set is hidden around the room. Each player is given a card and has to find the identical partner. When he has found it, he returns to the leader and is given another card. The player who finds the most cards is the winner. This game can also be played with one player.

Mailing a letter.   Prepare a mail box with a slit in the side and two sets of identical cards (pictures or words). Hold up a card and the player must find an identical card and put it in the box. This can be played as a race if there are two players.

Sorting games.   Several sets of identical cards are required for sorting games. The game is to see how quickly the player(s) can get them sorted into boxes.

Matching Games:
Non-Identical Matching

Instead of the pupil having to match identical pictures or words, he now has to match either a picture to a symbol accentuated word (SAW), or a SAW to a word printed in traditional orthography (TOW) or a picture with a word in TOW. All the above games—word pairs, bingo, dominoes, and so on—can be played with nonidentical matching as the pupil becomes more competent.

Recognition Games

Find the word.   The word cards are spread out on the floor. The dealer names a word and the player has to find it before the dealer (or another player) does. The winner is the one with the most cards. This can also be played with pictures.

Mailing a letter.   Prepare word cards or picture cards and also a mail box with a slit in it. Spread the cards on the table. The dealer names a card and the player(s) must find the card and put it in the box.

Bingo.   This is played as described above, but the dealer reads out a word instead of holding up a card for matching. If a player find this word on his card, he claims it and covers it up. The winner is the player who completes his card first.

Games for Reading or Recall

Wall game.   The word or picture cards are popped up from behind a box or "wall" for as short a time as possible for the player to identify them. This game is useful to increase reading speed.

Word skittles.   Word cards are propped up on stands and the game is to name one of the words and knock the correct one down with a ball.

Pick a card.   Rather like the procedure in a card trick, the dealer fans the word cards out in his hand, and the player then picks any card he chooses. In order to keep it, he must read it correctly, otherwise it is added to the dealer's pile. The player with the most cards wins.

Word spotting.   A board is made with a number of words printed on it, with each word printed on both sides of the board. Under each word is a hole. The leader reads out each word and the player has to stick a pencil through the appropriate hole. If two players with different levels of skill are playing together, pictures can be drawn above the holes on one side of the board instead of words.

Stepping stones.   Word cards are scattered on the floor and the player has to "cross the river" by stepping on each word and reading what it says.

Robbers.   Word cards are spread on the table or floor. The players read each card in turn and then shut their eyes, while the leader removes one card. The players open their eyes and then have to guess which card is gone. If they are correct, they claim it.

Fishing games.   Make a number of cardboard fish with words printed on them. A paper clip is slipped on to each fish's nose. Attach a magnet to the end of a model fishing line. Each player then fishes out of the pond (large box). He is allowed to keep his catch if he can read the word printed on it. The player with the most fish wins.

Read and do.   Action flash cards are held up, one at a time with the words *stand*, *sit*, *talk*, and *hop* printed on them. The players have to read the card and do whatever is printed on it.

Read and find.   Similar to the above, except that objects are scattered around the room and the words printed on the cards are the names of these objects. As each flash card is held up, the player(s) must find the appropriate object.

Treasure hunt. Word or sentence cards are hidden strategically around the house or room. Each card leads to the next, and each is either a one-word clue, such as *drawer* (the next card is hidden in the drawer) or a sentence, such as *look under the mat.* A prize is hidden in the last hiding place.

Dominoes. This game is played with word dominoes, and the player must read the word before placing his domino or he misses a turn.

Bingo. This game is played with cards to be filled up as before, but the player must read the card that the dealer holds up before claiming it for his card.

First to the shop

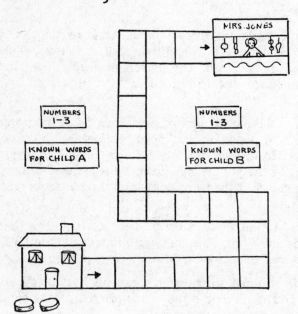

Child A takes top word from pile and reads it and then takes top card from number pile to see how many squares to move counter. Child B repeats the sequence using his known words.

MORE DIFFICULT GAMES

Word race game. A simple board game using dice and counters, and requiring the player(s) to read words already in their word-bank. Symbol accentuated (SAW) "prompt" cards may be used in times of difficulty.

First to the store. This can be played with two students with different words in their word banks. The player picks the top word from his pile and reads it, and then picks a card from the number pile to see how many squares to move his counter. The second player does the same, using a different pile of words.

Land on the word. This can be played with two students. Student A throws the dice and moves a marker along the word track. If he can read the word he has landed on, he removes that word and replaces it with another. Student B repeats the sequence. The child with the most words wins the game.

LAND ON THE WORD

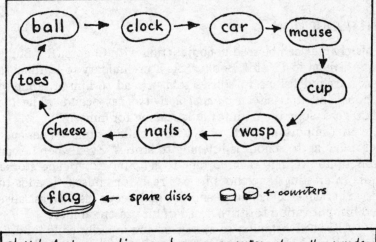

6

Listening to stories

INTRODUCTION

This chapter can be read in conjunction with Chapter 8, "Building a Bridge to Printed Books." As a preliminary to learning to read, a child listens to stories told or read to him at home or school, and it is also a *parallel* activity that occurs while the child goes along the path towards reading for himself.

An important part of a young child's home experience before going to school is listening to stories. Even when he can read quite well, it is important to let him experience stories more interesting than those he can read for himself. It adds to his experience of language and life and keeps his interest alive and his motivation to strive ahead of his present ability.

Although listening to stories occurs in early childhood, it happens later too. Adults listen to stories and dramas on radio and TV. In Colonial times, reading aloud in families was common. Earlier still, balladeers told their tales in villages and markets. Much of this oral experience was given without books.

Many mentally handicapped children find it hard to listen for any length of time. They can be helped both at home and in school. First we have to ensure that they *are* listening. How can we tell?

LISTENING

Listening is not the same as hearing. Most of us have sometimes been accused (or have accused others) of "not listening." What is the evidence for listening and not listening? Most teachers and parents are familiar with the half-glazed stare that means the children are quiet but not fully attending.

It looks quite different from the stilling of movement and the alert gaze of a group that are fully absorbed in the spoken word. It is very difficult to explain *how* it is different. Yet, commonly, human beings can easily recognize the difference. Hence the accusation: "You're not listening!"

Here are some cues—they are taken from the observed behavior of "listeners" and "non-listeners."

SUGGESTS LISTENING	SUGGESTS NOT LISTENING
1. Startles and turns to source of sound.	Continues activity without change.
2. Responds with appropriate action when told to do something.	Responds with inappropriate action, or no response.
3. Responds with appropriate words (or substitute mime) to conversation.	Responds with inappropriate replies or none, or (in case of sophisticated adult) non-committal murmur.
4. Becomes still, reducing restless body movements and vocalization.	Continues restless movements in solitary fashion or pokes others.
5. Interjects questions or offers relevant information	Interjects irrelevant speech or noise, or chooses another activity and goes away.

To sum it all up, listening is an active process, and, for our children, the problem is two-fold:

1. how can we catch their attention?
2. how can we keep it?

We have to remember that most of them (whatever their chronological age) will not exceed a mental age of four or five and will show some, but not all, of the characteristics of much younger children. How is *their* attention caught and held? It helps if the child has had the pleasure that a person can give with a picture book at home.

READING TO YOUR CHILD FROM PICTURE BOOKS

We do not always realize how much a child learns from sharing picture books with an adult. At first, the book will be one with pictures only. The shared experience of learning to recognize the pictures and hear about them is teaching the child to love books, to handle them carefully, and to turn the pages. More important still is the language learning that takes place in these sessions and the introduction to new ideas and to new names of objects. In fact, looking at books is teaching him to associate pictures with real objects. *Picture Words for Beginners*, by Milton Bradley, contains many hints on how to make the most of early picture books with the slow learning child, or indeed with any young child.

It is important to start showing the child picture books early. At first he may have such a short attention span that it may seem barely worthwhile. You should persevere, but make sure that you turn it into a special treat. This should be a time when both you and the child are relaxed—traditionally, it is often bedtime. At first, the sessions should be very short. A good rule of thumb is to put the book away *before* the child loses interest, not after. He may protest, but in this way he will look forward to the next day's treat. Gradually lengthen the time you spend together looking at books.

Furthermore, it is not only the mother who can share this experience with her child. The father and the grandparents are often very good at it, as are brothers and sisters. Later on, similar activities can go on in school when teachers or their helpers read to the child in the classroom.

In a later chapter (Chapter 8), we shall make some suggestions about ways in which this reading time can best be structured so that the child can get the most out of it, and perhaps set out on the path of reading for himself.

Without realizing, it he will learn a great deal as a result of these sessions. But he will learn much more if you are both enjoying it and if you resist the temptation to turn this time into a lesson period. It is essential that the child be allowed to learn at his own pace. Some children's progress will be fairly rapid and that of others will be so slow as to be almost imperceptible. For all children, it is important to give them time to gain absolute confidence and to practice and overlearn each new skill so that they can enjoy their mastery over it before being pushed on to the next stage. You will have to use your own judgment about this, but remember that reading is such an easy, automatic skill for most of us that we forget how complex and difficult it really is. If you are not careful, you may get impatient with a child who tends to forget what he knew the day before. Unless you curb this impatience, it will be picked up by the child and sap his confidence.

Choice of Books

There is a very wide choice of picture books suitable for the younger child, but a very limited choice for the older child or the young adult. Be guided by the individual child's interests and preferences and also by your own (you have to enjoy the sessions as well as he, your enthusiasm will rub off onto the child). At the end of this book (Bibliography), you will find a list of recommended books, but they are suggestions only, and the list is not exhaustive.

STORY TELLING
WITHOUT BOOKS

Not all the stories that children hear come from books. It is a different experience hearing a story that is told—a warm family experience—because we can put in details that are private to the child. Many famous children's books were first told to children in this way *(Alice in Wonderland, Winnie-the-Pooh,* and *The Hobbit).*

We (teachers and parents) cannot aspire to be geniuses at story telling. All we need to remember is that children (like other people) enjoy hearing about themselves; they like to hear the same story more than once; they like action; they like to laugh; they like reality mixed up with a bit of fantasy. A story can be made of nothing!

Here is an example taken from ordinary family experience.

A four-year-old (David) was being tiresome, bored, and whining. Now he was always fascinated with garbage cans, the men, and their trucks. So one day his mother said, "If you don't stop it, David, I'll put you in the garbage can and shut the lid!" (Pulling a face and speaking in a story-book way to show it was fantasy.) "And then," she went on, "the garbage-men came and picked up the can and said, 'My word, that's heavy.'" "Did they put me in the truck?" asked David. "Yes, and the driver jumped in the cab and drove off. Brr-Brr-Brr." "Did I get to the dump?" "Yes, but the garbage men saw your new hat sticking out, and they found you and drove back here. There they are at the door now!" David ran to the door, and opened it and mother and son said (to the invisible callers), grinning at each other, "Thank you."

David asked for this story many times. It has David in it, he does something, and he thinks it's funny—he can listen better because he participates. The repetition of the story makes him more confident of his part.

Most of us have been to a pantomime and noticed how the actors get the young audience shouting warnings to the silly lady who cannot see the wolf creeping up behind. This idea has been adapted to both classroom and home in the story of the Birthday Party.

Story One: Jane's Birthday Party

This is centered on a real party, and it can be performed at home with guests: Jane (who, let us say, fifteen), Mom and Dad, brother and sister, friend; or at school with classmates, teachers, helpers, or other adults. It is a real occasion and there is a cake and candles. Perhaps we begin with "Happy Birthday." Then into the story:

> It was Jane's birthday, and we all sang "Happy Birthday Jane," and clapped (action). Then Mom brought in the cake (cake brought in). "It should have fifteen candles," said Jane. "It has," said Mom. "Now, nobody touch it while I go for orange juice. Will you all tell me if anybody touches it? Will you?" (Children: "Yes!" Mom goes out.)
>
> (Dad tiptoes to cake, grins and winks, and elaborately hides one candle. "Don't tell!" he whispers, fingers to lips. Then he stands apart. Reenter Mom.)
>
> Children shout and betray Dad who promises not to do it again.
>
> This episode is repeated to ensure participation until few candles are left. But watch for restlessness, and end it before boredom sets in (among children, not adults). Restore candles and end story thus: "And so Jane said to everyone 'Come and sit down. You sit here John, you here Mary,'" etc. The party then proceeds.

Note the resemblance to the pantomime technique and the repetition.

As there are several children in a class, and possibly siblings at home, the game can become familiar. It lends itself to repetition and variations.

Warning note: Do not use the game to teach a number concept of fifteen. This is too irrelevant to the purpose and spoils the essential thrust of the project.

Story Two: The Car

Tom's father runs a garage and allows sixteen-year-old Tom to help a little. He knows about cars, especially the components of a repair job. This story is about him and for him. The teacher or parent needs to make sure to get the details correct, as he or she may be more ignorant than Tom.

One day, Tom's father said, "Tom that car outside is heading for a crash. It's going too fast and that corner's dangerous." (Sounds of speeding car followed by CRASH.) "Tom, call the police. Ask for the ambulance." Tom picked up the phone and dialed 411. (The story continues with simple dialogue on the phone.) Then Tom and his father got the tow truck and towed the wrecked car in. The windshield was smashed, the steering wheel buckled ... (Details follow of the damage). The rest of the story has Tom and his father working together on the repair, talking of tools and car parts as they work.

Since Tom is in the story, he can participate and add to or change details as he wishes. It can be acted out at any point. It can be taped so that Tom can listen until he has it by heart. If it is taped, sound effects should be included. If Tom records his own contributions, it can be later used for a reading text as part of the language-experience approach. But for the time being, its use is as a story and the training of Tom to be an active listener.

Adaptation to the Classroom

A story like this can be invented for each member of the class. In the school situation there are various extensions of the idea. For instance, the class stories can be written or typed to make a classbook that can be illustrated, possibly with photographs, and read to the class. It can later become a text for reading by those pupils advanced enough for early reading. Each pupil can begin by reading his own story and then progress to reading those of his friends. The exercise can be, and should be, repeated until the stories are very familiar.

Story Three: A Family Trip

Not all stories have to be long. This one can be told after a trip to the zoo.

Jane and Mom and Dad and Billy and I went to the zoo. And we saw a huge elephant. Billy was frightened, but Jane said, "Can I have a ride?" The elephant liked Dad's pipe and tried to smoke it! Billy liked the monkeys best. The big bear had a baby bear. We had tea at the restaurant, and Jane ate more cookies than anybody else. Mom said, "You'll be sick, Jane." But she wasn't.

It does not really matter if this is literally true, as long as it nearly is!

Story Four

Here is another very short story. (This one arose out of a picture in a magazine—it had quite a different text.)

> Jane and Mary are in their jeans. They are dancing to records at the disco.

**Story Five: Action Story
in the Classroom:
The Lost Princess**

This story is based on a story for seven-year-old children about an Indian girl who strayed into the forest from the wigwam and got lost. Her friends looked for her but could not find her. Then one of the braves saw her necklace and put his ear to the ground to listen. He could hear her running. So they all shouted, and the girl called back. So, eventually, after searching everywhere, they found her.

The aim was to give the pupils experience of listening to a story and turning it into action, and it was adapted. Two prepositions, *between* and *behind*, were fitted into the story. For instance, here is one sentence from the story the teacher read:

> The lost princess called and called, the Indians went between the rocks and between the trees, looking for her. At last they found her, sitting behind the little pine tree on the hill.

> Everyone was happy that she had been found, and they sang as they ran home, going between the trees of the great forest.

The whole story was told to the group, and they were shown a picture of wigwams in an Indian village. They were given headbands and feathers, and stools and chairs and blankets were used to represent wigwams and trees and rocks.

The students showed themselves that they were able to conceive these "props" imaginatively and, indeed, added to the story-line. John, for instance, said he (as an Indian brave) would go hunting for dinner. Hilda said she would cook and wash. Jimmy said he would take his bow and arrow. Mary said she was sad about the lost princess but would make dinner for her when she came back. Peter, who had little or no spoken language, got up and demonstrated a war-dance.

Apart from these additions, the students followed the story-line. It is not just a rough and tumble Indian game, but an action-story that needs careful preparation of the children by the adults, and careful active listening by the children.

Other Action Stories

In case invention fails, it is always possible to go back to traditional action stories—such as Simon Says. Here is one very old illustrated story, one that gives a link with body image. The art is first done by the adult, and then given to the child to do.

One day mom went shopping. She bought an apple, with a bad spot in it:

Then she bought another apple with a bad spot in it:

Then she bought a pear:

Then she bought a banana:

Then she bought a bag and some string to tie it up:

And that's Mom who went shopping!

The drawings are done as the story is told. Notice that they do not have to be good drawings!

STORIES READ FROM BOOKS

It is not easy to find the right books to read. The first books should have clear, uncluttered, and attractive pictures of familiar objects and events. The captions under the pictures should be in clear, large print, and there should be only one word under each picture. Later books may have a sentence under each picture. Eventually, you will be reading whole stories. Don't forget we are still talking about your reading to the child. In Chapter 8 we shall discuss how we can get the child to begin reading for himself.

Suggestions for Choosing Books to Read to Students at Home and in the Classroom

The books and stories should be capable of becoming favorites. We would like the child to know the stories almost by heart so that he complains if the reader reads it wrong!

They will then become part of our student's store of experience. Books will become familiar and will be associated with pleasure.

You will find a list of books at the end of the book. It is a highly selective list and is intended only as a guide. The first books are very simple picture books with captions or short texts. Many of the later ones are selections from well known infant or junior reading books, although we are not suggesting that the children should go through reading schemes. Many of the stories are folk tales with an element of fantasy or versions of children's classics. They are all illustrated in a timeless way and are probably a better investment than those illustrated to fit some current fashion. This is especially applicable to teenagers whose fashions change so quickly.

Some of the books in the list are already adapted in their texts. Others, such as those of Beatrix Potter, have accompanying film strips to help to present them. Other books have been excluded because the language in which they are written is too complex even for reading to our children—such as classics like *Alice in Wonderland* and some of the Beatrix Potter tales.

Even so, some of the books in the list may seem difficult. But their story-line is clear and can be followed by the listeners if the reader selects well, modifies the text, and is prepared to act a little. Finally, the selections from children's readers with their large, clear print and somewhat limited vocabulary are meant *to be read to the students*, not *by* them at this stage. We want the children to be familiar with them as favorite stories before reading them themselves. (We shall explain how we take this step in Chapter 8.) The ones we have chosen are worth reading aloud for their story-value. For instance, *Listening Time* (published by Bowman Records, Inc.) allows the child to hear the text while he is looking at the storybook. Adults can read aloud if they want to, but a recording is also available for the child. This in itself provides an important step for the child, from listening to a familiar adult reading in the close, cosy group of family unit or class, to reading on his own. The voice is familiar, the book in his hand is familiar, and he can, as he listens to the tape, follow voice and text together.

READING ALOUD TO TEENAGERS WITH TEENAGE INTERESTS

Magazines

There is some material in print that does not appeal to adults but that is important to children and young people. Comics and magazines that reflect teenage interests are examples. Children who can read spend a good deal of time on this material. It appeals to them for its own sake and also has an extra appeal because adults somewhat disapprove. So the question arises of whether we should help those teenagers who cannot read to have access to such material.

Our answer would be yes, because it is typical of normal development for teenagers to like current fashion, to adopt certain crazes, and to be in the know about popular music and its stars. They read magazines that cater to these tastes.

Handicapped teenagers are sometimes excluded from this scene in spite of wanting to join it. We can help them be more knowledgeable by reading to them aloud from their favorite magazines. It is for this reason that we have included a few magazines in the list of books for reading aloud.

It may be a good idea to give this job to those high school boys and girls who come into special schools to help, or to non-handicapped brothers and sisters. They will read with more enthusiasm!

Reading from Serious Books
that Cater to Interests
but are Difficult to Understand

Some books about hobbies come into this category, as do classic stories written indeed for the young but in a sophisticated style. It would be a pity if we excluded them from our reading matter. Here is a way of adapting them.

Do not read straight from the book, but edit, shorten, rephrase, and retell the story as you go along. With practice, this can be done easily, especially if the book is well known to you. Choose a classic book with a strong and vigorous story—one that does not depend on psychological interest but rather on action. Make sure it is well illustrated.

One good example is *Robinson Crusoe*. Written by Daniel Defoe, it was not meant for children but for the adult reader of the eighteenth century. Yet its action packed story has made it a favorite of children and adults.

It will not be possible to read *Robinson Crusoe* straight from its text because its language is too complex and strange. But the story can be told almost by talking about the pictures alone. All its episodes are full of easily understood detail: the shipwreck, the desert island, the raft, the building of the hut and stockade, the dog, the parrot, and the goats.

Tolkien's children's classic, *The Hobbit*, lends itself to a mixture of abridged telling and reading from the text. It is a book in which each chapter covers a part of the story that stands by itself. For instance, when Bilbo and the dwarves are well on their way, the weather turns bad, it rains, a pony slips into the river, and their food is lost. The dwarves are unable to light a fire. They see a light in the trees and send Bilbo to seek it out. All this can be retold in simple words. But at the climax of that adventure, you can read straight from the text:

> ... Three very large persons sitting round a very large fire of beech-logs. They were toasting mutton on long spits of wood, and licking the gravy off their fingers. There was a fine toothsome smell. Also there was a barrel of good drink at hand, and they were drinking out of jugs. But they were trolls. ...

> Mutton yesterday, mutton today and blimey, if it don't look like mutton again tomorrer, said one of the trolls.
>
> From *The Hobbit* by J. R. R. Tolkien.

Of course, there will be some words that are not understood. A little acting would help, and, naturally, some introduction to this world of trolls, dwarves, and dragons will be needed. But the language conveys an excitement missing from books for young readers, which seem dull and unmotivating to older children. Moreover, the harmless indecorousness of the text appeals to teenagers. That is why it is often better to read from classic books and retell them yourself than to get books that have already been adapted. What about this tremendous opening to a story by Hans Anderson—who could resist it?

> Left-right! Left-right! Down the country road came a soldier marching. Left-right! Left-right . . . he met an old witch on the road. Oh! she was ugly . . . Her lower lip hung down on her chest.
>
> From "The Tinder Box."

Finally, one book in our list, written by a mentally handicapped teenager, is well worth reading aloud. This is *The World of Nigel Hunt*.

In this chapter we have been describing adults reading to children. In the following chapters (7 and 8), we explore methods for stimulating progress into independent reading.

7

Word families

INTRODUCTION

A useful way to build up knowledge is to go from the known to the unknown. For instance, the botanist will be very familiar with the daisy before he discovers the details of its flower structure, habit of growth, and habitat. The artist, if he tries to draw a familiar object like a spoon, will soon discover that he does not know as much about it as he once thought and will have to study each curve and indentation.

By the time ordinary children come to school, we can assume that they are already familiar with words and letters and that we can build on this foundation. With mentally handicapped children, we have to pay much more attention to pre-reading skills and build them up step by step. This is what the preceding chapters have been about. Once this has been done we are on more familiar ground. Many books have been written about the stages of learning to read that will be described in this chapter, and we shall suggest some that you may like to read for further information.

However, a word of warning. Because this chapter is where we might begin with ordinary children, it is not where we should begin with handicapped children who have not built up the necessary prereading skills. We suggest that you do not attempt this chapter until your child has a sight vocabulary of *at least* thirty words that he can confidently read and recognize.

Then he will be ready to find out more about these already familiar words and make finer discriminations about them. He will be ready to learn about the similarities between words and the subtle differences that are vital to their recognition.

For maximum learning to take place at this stage, close cooperation between teachers and parents is ideal. In this team we would also include speech therapists when we are dealing with children who have problems discriminating speech sounds and problems in articulation.

Teachers will find nothing startlingly new in this chapter, but if they are dealing with a learning disabled child for the first time, they should note the orientation and the programing of each stage.

Parents have a vital part to play. Not only will their interest and involvement increase their child's, but they will ensure, through playing word games, that the child will build a solid foundation on which to learn more, and that the child will practice his newly learned skills until they become automatic.

Speech therapists have an expert knowledge of the child's ability to hear the differences between sounds and ability to form the necessary speech sounds. Their advice in the order of the stages will be invaluable.

For all concerned, do not stress your roles as teachers, but stress the child's role as a learner. Be ready at each stage to reverse roles so that the child becomes the leader in a teaching game. Provide the opportunity for the child to check himself so that he becomes increasingly independent. Do not be too eager to jump in and help him. Because many handicapped children are slow to react, we tend to believe that they are less able than they actually are. It is essential to give them time.

Now for some practical suggestions:

AUDITORY DISCRIMINATION

Before taking the next step in learning to read, a child has to learn to listen more exactly to the sounds that go together to form words and to distinguish between those that are the same and those that are different. The traditional game of "I Spy" is excellent practice for distinguishing the initial letters of words. This game leads a child, step-by-step, to the point where he is able to join in with the traditional game, and it also teaches him, systematically, to recognize the initial letter sounds.

In the game as we play it, the letter sounds are always presented in the context of words and never in isolation as in traditional "I Spy" where the player says, "I spy with my little eye something beginning with B," using the letter name and not giving very many clues as to the word pronunciation. Instead of using the letter names, some people play this game using the so called letter sounds, but it is very difficult to pronounce the *sound* of the consonants (b, c, d, f, g, etc.) without adding an intrusive -*ee* sound on the end so that we say "bee," "cee," "dee." This makes guessing more difficult. So in our version, we make it easier for the child by sounding the first vowel sound as well as the first consonant sound of each word; *bu*— for *bun*, *wi*— for *window* and so on.

Program for the Game
"I Spy" or "Guess What I am Going to Say"

Stage one. Collect a few objects or pictures to make guessing easier, and put these where the child can see them easily. Tell him he has to guess which one you are going to say. Make sure that each object begins with a different letter sound at this stage—*milk*, *butter*, and *coffee*. Do not choose any objects that begin with the same letter—*mug* and *milk*. Change the objects and pictures when you play the game again, but avoid words that are difficult to discriminate from one another. Do not have words beginning with the sounds *c*, *t*, *d*, and *g* together in the same game (or *p* and *b*, or *v*, *f*, and *th*, or *l*, *r*, *w*, and *y*) as these letter sounds are difficult to tell apart when spoken.

This game is training your child's discrimination, and, as

114

he learns to listen, you can start to introduce these more difficult sounds.

How to Play

Sit in front of the toys or pictures and say either, "I spy with
my little eye something that begins with . . . . See if you can
guess what it is."

OR, a simpler version, "What am I starting to say?" When
your child is familiar with the game, reverse roles and let him
get *you* guessing.

Stage two.   Introduce a few more objects, including one or
two that have the same initial consonant sound but a different
vowel sound, such as *ca(t)* and *cu(p)* or *mi(lk)* and *ma(t)*.

Stage three.   Start to introduce some of the finer sound discriminations, such as those starting with *c, t, d, g,* but do this
gradually. Put them together only when they have been
recognized separately at stage one. Do not introduce them all at
once, although *p-b* discrimination can be introduced here.

Stage four.   Gradually introduce the sound discrimination
between *v, f, th,* and, last of all *l, r, w,* and *y.* You may find that
when you reverse roles, your child has difficulty in getting his
tongue around these sounds and confuses them. Your speech
therapist can advise on how far to go and which sounds to
choose.

Stage five.   Introduce initial consonant blends—words such as
sprou(t)s, stri(ng), and *screw(s).* Instead of preparing a special
collection of pictures in order to play the game, you can now
name objects round the room or seen from the car.

The Parson's Cat

This is a traditional game that most people have played in
childhood. In case you do not know it, this is how it is played.
A letter of the alphabet is chosen, usually *a* first and then *b,*
and so on. The order can be varied, and each player has to think
of an adjective starting with that letter. Thus the parson's cat is
a *black* cat or a *brown* cat. Small children and handicapped

children may find this game too difficult to play in its traditional form. Their repertoire of adjectives is likely to be limited, and they may find it hard to think of one out of the blue.

Here is a simpler version. Draw and cut out a number of cats and color them different colors. Make some big and some little, some hairy and some smooth, and some smiling and some cross. Use these to help your child in playing the game.

Rhyming Words

In this game, one player says a word. The next child says a word that rhymes with it—*cat* and *bat*. You will probably have to prompt your child until he gets the idea.

Syllables

Start this game with compound words such as *handbag*, *postman*, *matchbox*, and *briefcase*. You say the word. Your child has a stick and a drum or can on which to beat out the number of syllables. You may have to demonstrate it at first.

To begin with, contrast words with only one syllable and those with two. Later, introduce words with more than two syllables. As well as tapping out the syllables, your child can also count how many there are.

VISUAL DISCRIMINATION

The Word Bank: Initial Letter Sounds

In the previous chapters, we have suggested that as the child's sight vocabulary grows, the words he knows should be added to a word bank (this can be a box or filing box). Alphabetical card dividers should now be added to this word bank with the letters of the alphabet clearly printed on them. A picture can be added that represents a word beginning with that letter. Some more suggestions on introducing the alphabet will be included at the end of this chapter. As soon as your child has acquired a sight vocabulary of ten to thirty words, he should be helping you sort them by initial letter and put them back into his word bank.

Finding two alike. You will have to wait until your child has acquired a word bank of thirty or forty words before you show him similarities in the endings of words and sorting his word bank into families.

For instance, he may have the name *Pat* in his bank. Now help him to find *cat* and *mat* and *rat*. Do this with more difficult words such as *light*, *sight*, *right*. Put a few words on the table and play a game. Hold one up and ask him to find one belonging to the same family.

Adding to the family. You will probably find that your child has not many examples of each word family in his word bank, so now is the time to show him how he can add to the word family. For instance, if he already knows the word *and*, show him how to make the words *hand*, *sand*, and *band*, by altering the initial letter. Make a duplicate set of words belonging to different word families, and let him sort them out into pockets made of envelopes stuck on to a card and fastened on the wall. The envelopes should be clearly marked with one example of the family on the outside. Give him plenty of practice in sorting his words into families.

At this stage all the word families should arise out of the words your child already knows. If he has practice in playing the rhyming game, this will help him a great deal at this stage and you will be able to get him to think of new words which belong to the same family as the key word. You may have to discard some of the words he thinks of because, although they rhyme with the key word, they are spelled differently; e.g., *tale* and *sail*.

GAMES TO PLAY

Make a Word

A key word, such as *and*, *at*, *it*, *old*, or *ice*, is placed in the middle of the table. Each player has an identical set of single-letter cards, such as *b, c, d, f, g h, l, m, n, p, r, s, t,* and *v.*

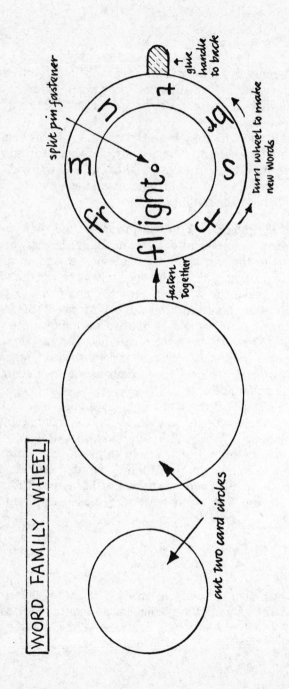

WORD FAMILY WHEEL

cut two card circles

fasten together

split pin fastener

glue handle to back

turn wheel to make new words

fl ight

fr
m
n
t
br
s
t

Each player, in turn, has to place a single letter in front of the key word to make a new word such as *nice* and *rice*.

Players are required to read the words they have made and if it is a real word they gain a point.

Word Family Wheel

The illustration shows you how to make a word family wheel. In this game each player turns the wheel so that a new word appears, and, to gain a point, he must read the word. Children often like to use the wheel on their own as well as in the game, and this should be encouraged.

Word Family Strip

The illustration below shows you how to make a word family strip.

WORD FAMILY STRIP

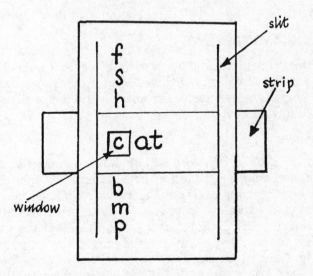

This is a variation on the word family wheel and can be used by the child on his own or in a game.

Split Page Books

This illustration shows you how to make a split page book.

This book can be used either in a game or for individual practice.

WRITING AND SPELLING

Collecting words into families is a great help in learning how to spell. For the child with sufficient motor control to form the letters himself, these families can now be used in a spelling game in the following way.

Trace and Say

One of the shorter key words should be chosen, such as *at*, and this letter should be printed in large letters. The child is then shown how to trace over the letters with his finger or with a piece of thin paper and a pencil. While he traces, he says the word slowly, "*at.*" It is important not to distort the word in any way, but to merely draw out the sounds. Having traced the word, he turns the master copy over and tries to write the word on a separate sheet without looking. He then checks his word with the master copy and, if it is wrong, traces over again. The pupil should be given some way of recording his own progress. His aim will be to spell the word correctly in the shortest number of trials.

Once the pupil is able to spell *at* without mistakes, he adds another letter to it to spell, for example, *hat*. The child then follows the same procedure, tracing the word and saying it slowly as he traces with his finger or a pencil, and then writing the word without a copy. Care should be taken to ensure that the pupil forms his letters correctly and the right way round.

A child, who for any reason is not able to write, can also *learn* to spell if he is given individual letter cards that he puts in the correct order by matching them with the master copy and then tries without the copy in front of him and sees how quickly he can learn to spell the word. In the case of a child with a physical handicap, the teacher can either trace with her finger around the letters of the word and slowly say the word, or she can guide his finger around if he is not too handicapped. For these children, it often helps to make a series of letter shapes covered with fabric or with sand paper so that the letter shapes can be easily felt.

This is particularly useful for the sight-impaired child. He may also form the letters in damp sand with his finger or with a stick.

Zig-Zag Spelling Aid

The drawing on the next page shows how to make a zig-zag spelling aid.

This will be extremely useful when you choose a word with more than three letters. Again, the child can check himself by unfolding the zig-zag book at each stage, adding the missing letters and then checking with the master copy.

Practice Spelling Game

This game gives your pupil further practice in writing the word families he has already learned. It also is a memory game and helps his powers of observation. For this game you will need a blackboard that will wipe clean.

Robbers

The leader in the game (the teacher to start with, but later on the roles can be reversed) prints a few words from any one word family on the board, and the player reads them as they are

ZIG-ZAG SPELLING AID

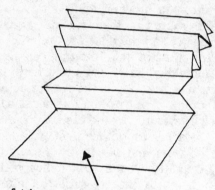

fold paper strip into zig-zag

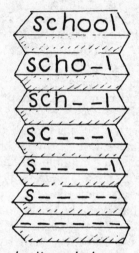

gradually omit letters of the word.

being printed. The leader then asks the player to shut his eyes (depending on the age of the pupil, this can be built up into a piece of fantasy, saying it is night time and robbers may be about). While the pupil's eyes are shut, one of the words is rubbed off the board and the pupil must guess what it was, and then, having guessed correctly, must put it back by printing it on the board.

This game should be introduced step by step:

Step 1. Only two words are written on the board.

Step 2. Four words are written on the board, but two of them are duplicates.

Step 3. The number of words on the board is gradually increased, but, for ease in spelling, they all belong to the same word family.

Step 4. Words from two word families are written on the board.

Step 5. A mixture of several word families is used.

Kim's Game

A tray is prepared on which there are a few word cards, which the pupil has already learned how to spell. The pupil is given time to look at the tray and read each word. The tray is then covered with a cloth and the pupil tries to write down all the words he remembers.

This is a difficult memory game if a lot of words are included, so it is best to program it, starting with only *one* word and then increasing the number to two, then to three, and so on.

You should start with short, easy words and go on to words that are longer and more difficult.

Variation of Kim's Game

Kim's game can also be played with little objects or toys as purely a memory game. It is probably best to play it in this way first so that the pupil has a chance to get the hang of the game before introducing the added task of having to write the words.

Hangman

More practice in spelling and recognizing words can be given with the traditional game of hangman.

One player begins by drawing a row of crosses on the paper to represent the number of letters in a word. He provides clues to help the other player to guess what the word might be: "It's an animal."

The second player then names a letter that he thinks might be in the word. (If he does not yet know the names of letters he selects one from a printed alphabet). If the letter is one of those in the word, the first player prints it in the right place under the word. If not, the first player starts to build a "gallows" (see opposite). And so it goes on, with one player continuing to guess the letters of the word until he has them all correct or, if he wishes, guessing the whole word before it is completed.

Here again, it is important to reverse roles and allow your child to be hangman.

You may have to simplify this game at first, not only by

giving a very short word as an example, but also by giving the guesser a limited choice of letters to choose from instead of the whole alphabet.

This might seem a somewhat heartless game, but most young people seem to enjoy it and will work hard in order to avoid being "hanged."

Crossword

Very simple crossword puzzles help in practicing spelling.

Workbooks

Once your child is able to spell a number of words, he will probably enjoy working through some of the good workbooks that are on the market. Check with your child's teacher for workbook suggestions.

Using Your Skill

There is little point in learning to spell just for its own sake. The skill should be put to use once it is acquired. Your child can help to label goods around the house or his own possessions. He can now help to write his own captions in his books and also start writing letters or cards to his family and friends.

He should also be encouraged to use his skill in order to make his own shopping list, to list the ingredients he will need for cooking, or to make lists of things connected with his hobbies: *Birds I have seen, or cars I have seen.*

He will now be able to start to help you by making a shopping list for you when you tell him what items you need.

COVERING MORE GROUND

Once your pupil has become proficient in reading and writing word families that have arisen from familiar words in his word bank, he will be ready for a more systematic program to help him read books that he has not seen before and to become familiar with the rules that apply to the written word. This will help him have an educated guess at new words.

It is not the purpose of this book to outline a detailed pro-

THE GAME OF HANGMAN

The first player (the hangman) thinks of a word
e.g. CAMEL and draws a cross for each letter.

$$\times \quad \times \quad \times \quad \times \quad \times$$

The second player guesses a letter, e.g. E or the
whole word. If the letter or word is right it is
written above the appropriate cross or crosses.

$$\times \quad \times \quad \times \quad \overset{E}{\times} \quad \times$$

If the letter or word is wrong the hangman starts to
build the gallows, one stage for each wrong guess.

STAGES OF BUILDING THE GALLOWS

Building the gallows Stages 1- 6 for each wrong
letter.

Hanging the man Stages 7-12 for following wrong
letters. To win the player must guess the word
before being hanged otherwise the hangman wins.

gram for this more advanced stage of learning to read. There are many excellent programs on the market that outline a systematic phonic approach. Some examples are listed in the Bibliography on page 147. This is by no means a comprehensive list and such programs are only suitable for a few children.

It is important at this stage that parents and teachers work together; or that parents concentrate on the *use* of reading skills, and leave their extension to the school.

Not all pupils will reach this stage but they may be prepared for the work in Chapter 8 if certain regular words are taught. The following games will prove helpful.

Digraph Tins

Old coffee cans are very useful for this game. Each child has an empty can and a chart is put up on the wall marked out into two-inch squares with a digraph (common two-letter combination) printed in each square. Duplicate two-inch cards are made for each child (these are more durable if they are laminated). The child is given the appropriate card to put in his can whenever a new digraph is encountered or learned. Commonly occurring digraphs are: *ea, ee, ay, ai, oy, oi, ar, or, er, ir, ur, ow, aw, oa, sh, ch,* and *th.*

These are learned by finding them in familiar words. For example, the student knows the word *sea,* so you show him that by covering up the *s* you get the sound *ea.* Once a child has put one or two digraphs in his can, you can begin to play games with them. Here are a few suggestions:

Find a Match

The teacher sounds one of the digraphs and points to it on the chart. The student lays out his cards in front of him and finds one to match.

Which Is This?

The teacher now says a whole word—*boy*—and the student has to find the appropriate digraph from his collection, in this case *oy.* If the child has difficulty, the teacher then indicates and sounds out the correct digraph on the chart.

At first, this game should be played with a very limited choice of one or two cards. More cards should be added only when the child is certain of these others. Later, he will find these digraph cans very useful in helping him to spell. Children who use this means of reference are able to become increasingly independent of the teacher.

Consonant blends. Similar games can be played with consonant blends, such as *st* (as in *stop*), *sp* (as in *speak*), *sl* (as in *slow*), *sn* (as in *snow*), *sc* (as in *scale*), *sm* (as in *smile*), *sn* (as in *snack*), *pr* (as in *proud*), *pl* (as in *place*), and *tr* (as in *tree*). Blends of more than two consonants are more difficult and should be left until later, such as *str* (as in *string*).

Only examples of consonant blends occurring at the beginning of words should be introduced at this stage, and not those occurring at the end of words, such as *st* as in *best*.

More Games

Most of the games outlined in Chapter 5 can be adapted for use with digraphs and consonant blends. For instance, the game of dominoes can be played so that a digraph or consonant blend has to be matched with an appropriate picture—the digraph *oy* has to be matched with the picture of a boy or of a toy, Alternatively, the digraph can be matched with a whole word—the digraph *oy* has to be matched either with the word *toy* or *boy*.

Similarly, Bingo and Find the Partner can be adapted.

In fact, these word games form an integral part of the whole process and should be continued at every stage to ensure that learning is consolidated and internalized and can be applied to new situations.

Finally, any skill is liable to lapse if it is not used. This is particularly true of early reading. Every opportunity should be made for your child or teenager to use his newly acquired skill, and encouragement must not fade.

Building a bridge
to printed books

INTRODUCTION

When the child has a considerable number of words in his word bank and has begun to order and study them, as well as to read his own stories in a continuous text, see if he can read and get the message of continuous text in "cold" print.

We have left this chapter until the end of the book, because we think our students will need the "overlearning" we have described in earlier chapters before they can take the further steps in bridging the gap between their newly-acquired skills of word recognition and elementary word-attack skills and the more sophisticated skills required to read books with enjoyment and understanding, independently of adult help.

It is probably a bigger step for them than for young readers in primary schools who can rely on their considerable normally developed powers of generalization to help them to recognize new words just on the grounds of similarities to words they already know. Moreover, they have a large and growing spoken vocabulary and a growing competence in sentence structure that enables them to make intelligent guesses at what is coming next in a book, thus speeding up the process of mastering it.

All this is difficult for handicapped pupils. They will continue to need help before they can become independent readers. There will be a spread of ability; some will go faster than others; some will not go as far as others on the path to literacy.

But some will be able to go on to independent reading, because the activities described in earlier chapters will have helped them to acquire prereading and early reading skills on which to build.

Here, then, is the plan for building a bridge to printed books:

Foundations (See Chapters 1-7)	–recognition of words and letters –experience of books and stories –elementary word-attack skills –development of books from their own experience and language

The Bridge

–games with books familiar because they have been read aloud

"supported" reading of familiar books

"supported" reading of new books

Independent reading

books, magazines, and newspapers	printed messages in the environment

GUIDELINES

Guidelines on how to put this plan into operation follow.

1. Continue with the methods that gave the child experience of the pleasure of books. Even when he begins to read himself, he will be slow in getting enjoyment from it. It is important to run other activities—games and listening to stories—along-side those that follow.

2. *Play some games with the texts of the simplest books described in Chapter 6 (see list Appendix A).* The picture books with captions that have been used for reading aloud will be suitable, as are those with short clear text in bold print.

a. Read book, pausing before a key word and see if he will supply it.

b. Cover up one of the keywords with your fingers and get him to guess. Do this until he is good at it.

c. Next, you should print the caption under the first picture on a piece of paper. Place it under the picture to begin with, and let him "read" from your card instead of the printed page. Then show him the card without the picture to help him, and see if he can "read" it. Do this with each page of your picture book. When he is able to read all the captions without the pictures to help him, you should make a second strip of printed captions.

You will now have two strips for each printed page. Put one on the table and cut the other up into single words. Let him help you do this. Tell him what you are doing. Shuffle the words and then let him put them back in order by matching them with the second sentence strip. Let him practice doing this until he is good at it.

The next stage is to get him to put the words in order without the help of a model. Turn the sentence strip over so that he cannot see it while he is putting his words in the right order. Help him by reading the sentence slowly, word by word. When he has assembled the sentence, let him check himself by turning the sentence strip over. Give encouragement, but let him be as independent as possible. Do not try to correct his mistakes while he is working, but let him find them out by checking and then trying again. The aim is to enable him to play the game by himself and get very proficient at it.

Once he can do one sentence, you can do the same thing with the rest of the sentences in the book (do not choose a book with too many pages).

By now you will have a collection of single words on cards, and it is time to play games with these so that he learns to recognize each word out of context. As you have named the words already many times, he may have no difficulty.

To test his recognition of words, start by playing a game with two or three and choose the ones he recognizes most easily. Place three target-word cards with three other words (distractors) on the table and say, "Find 'boy'." Praise him for speed of recognition. Do this with each word. Do not call out the "distractors."

3. Teach him to recognize words he will meet often in books. Words such as *the, and, but, is, me,* and *to* occur frequently in all books. They can be taught by methods described earlier. Incorporate them into word-recognition games. For instance, play Bingo, using Stage 3 and then Stage 4 (See Chapters 2 and 5).

4. Choose a simple "favorite" book and teach him the words he does not yet know that occur in it. If it has been read often to him, he will know it almost by heart and be able to anticipate. He will already have some words in his word bank. Check the word banks and teach the words that are not yet in it, using symbol accentuation (if necessary) and then fading it out.

Get him to read to you from the book, but be ready to supply any word he does not readily read.

Be careful not to give him the impression of failing.

Books he knows well, especially those folktales with much repetition, are suitable for this activity. He will be able to anticipate what is coming.

5. Introduce books familiar for the story but of which the student does not know each word. Such a book might be one of the early books mentioned in see Chapter 6.

    a. Allow student to "follow" the text as you (or a tape recorder) read it.

    b. Teach words (from one or two pages) that he does not know.

    c. Get him to read some of the story, but be ready to supply missing words.

6. A note on overlearning and generalization. The kind of reading described above is a step towards independence in reading. It is "supported" reading. It is important to use many books and give many repetitions until the student gets used to the task and is quite good at it.

It is also important to help him to generalize. He may find it difficult to recognize a word in small print when it has always been familiar to him in large print.

You can help him to do this by playing matching games (see Chapters 2 and 5) if you, for instance, pair large-print words with words cut out of the newspaper. "Find its little brother" would be a good name for this game.

7. Move on to "silent" reading. If the student shows some proficiency in "supported" reading aloud, give him a simple book, preferably familiar to him, and ask him, with the help of its pictures, to tell you its story. (Books like the *Sullivan Programed Reading* series are suitable.)

Do not expect a high standard of story telling. Accept mime and a few words. The important thing to know is, does he get the idea of the story?

Participate in his enjoyment, as adults do when they speak of a book or film they have enjoyed. *Talk* with him about the subject of the story.

SUITABLE BOOKS
FOR SUPPORTED OR SILENT READING

On the whole, we are not suggesting that students who get to this stage should be put on to a reading level and taken through it. But they can read books selected from levels.

Any book that arouses the student's interest and is written with a simple enough text is suitable.

We have suggested some of these in our own list and have referred to other lists in print. It is not possible to give an exhaustive list because so much depends on what the child himself finds interesting and comprehensible. The sentences in the books should not be involved, and the ideas must not be too sophisticated or abstract. The story should be lively, either full of fancy, full of humor or full of incident. Although the language should be simple and clear, it should not be too flat and dreary. Children are often taken with a measure of eloquence, which is perhaps why books like *The Hobbit* or the Bowmar books are so popular.

There are two special difficulties in finding suitable books, and one, alas, we have not been able to solve. The special interests of adolescent girls have never really been catered for. When they are young, books for boys and girls are very similar, and their interests coincide. Around the age of sixteen, this is no longer so, and there is a shortage of books for girls. However, there is also the *general* problem of the handicapped teenager who is developing teenage interests but cannot cope with the books that are published for this particular market.

In the next section, we present some ideas for finding suitable reading matter for teenagers to read for themselves.

SUITABLE BOOKS FOR TEENAGERS TO READ FOR THEMSELVES

It is difficult to find books that fit both the interests and the levels of understanding of handicapped teenagers. Some reading books have been published with slow learners in mind, but many of these are too sophisticated in content for our pupils. (Consult the lists in the Bibliography, advocated in Chapter 6, for these.)

Hence, we suggest the following:

1. See if you can get books that illustrate the kind of activity your student is interested in. Choose a simple text, and help him to master it *and* to carry out its instructions. (Even with simple texts, you may need to modify the one provided; at least you are demonstrating that books help activities.)

2. Get simple nonfiction texts that reflect the pupil's interests (see Chapter 6) and support his reading of these as before.

3. Get magazines that reflect his interests and support his reading of these.

4. Help him to read the pages of a popular daily paper (sports or fashion pages) each day.

5. The environment itself is a "book" containing many printed messages that tell us what to do (or not to do). The environment, then, produces reading experiences. For instance, at the time of the year when we are writing this (Christmas) all kinds of important social messages abound. Christmas cards arrive in batches. Quite commonly, either inside or outside, they bear the same message, *Merry Christmas*, in different kinds of print. They often contain doggerel verse using the word *Christmas* in fancy print. They are signed with names of friends or relations, names with meaning to the teenager in the family. On the store window is a big notice: *Order your pumpkin pies now. Closed Christmas Day, and New Year's Day.* The Post Office gives the latest times for mailing letters and parcels. Appeals for charities come in unsealed envelopes to the house. Christmas is a time when reading and writing is a real social activity. The teenager in the family can be encouraged to use his reading skills to join in, possibly guessing the sender of each card as it comes and sending one of his own, perhaps to Grandma and Granddad.

Other times of the year have their special effect on reading skills, but opportunities for reading are always present in the environment.

Here is a selection of instructions in print that you can help teenagers read and understand:

To open, press here and pull back.
Open other side.
Keep medicines away from children.
External use only.

A bigger reading "demand" is in cooking recipes. All of these are experienced in day-to-day living. Outside, there are street signs, bus destinations and numbers, destinations on railway and subway stations.

The children who do not acquire the taste or skill for reading books can still use their word- and letter-recognition skill on the reading that abounds in the environment.

Remember that progress is likely to be slow, but it will be there. One way to ensure that you (teacher or parent) notice progress is to record it. In the next chapter, we present ideas for speedy and efficient recording of progress.

9

Recording progress

INTRODUCTION

It is important to keep a record of the student's progress. This is first and foremost for your own sake. Our memories are often not as reliable as we like to think, and, when progress is slow, we may not realize that it is taking place at all. We may be needlessly pessimistic.

Second, it is only through keeping records that we can see whether our teaching method is being successful so that it can be adjusted accordingly.

Third, when a pupil moves from one class to another, or from school to Adult Training Center or Further Education College, it is essential that detailed records should go with him.

Fourth, consistency will only come about if records are kept both at school, ATC or WAC, and at home.

Another good reason for keeping records is so that the young person himself can gain in confidence by seeing his own wealth of knowledge grow.

Keeping records need not be a chore, and we shall suggest

two levels of record keeping: a simple way of keeping an on-
going record (which can be used by parents and teachers or the
young person themselves) and a more formal method of record
keeping for school use or for use in research. These can be later
transferred to a graph and any acceleration of learning or learning plateau will be highlighted.

ONGOING RECORDS

The main method of keeping records is by means of a *Word
Bank*. An alphabetically arranged filing box is prepared with a
stock of cards. Each new word that reaches the required
criterion is filed in the box. If the date is written on the back of
each word card, this box will provide a record of progress, and
the information can be transferred to a formal record when
required.

Not only this, but the student will be able to see his skills
increase in a tangible way and should be allowed to count his
cards.

Rules for entry of words into the word bank should be
strict. The words in the word bank should be systematically
revised at intervals so that a record can be kept of the student's
retention of learning.

If required, each time a word is revised a new date can be
entered on the back of each card and a cross put beside it.

The student can learn to sort out the word cards alphabetically and place them correctly behind the alphabetical
dividers in the box. This recognition of initial letters and
letter sounds is a big step forward in independent reading.

If the dividers are marked with both traditional letters and
pictorial letters (see Chapter 1), this will be an additional help.

Games can also be played that will help your student listen
to initial letter sounds (see Chapter 1). To start with, not all the
words in the word bank need to be in traditional orthography.
Once a word is known in its accentuated form, it can go in the
word bank and be credited to the student in this form. The
traditional printed word will be written on the back of each
card, and once this has been learned, it will be credited to the

student, who will also be able to turn the card over if he forgets and requires extra cues.

FORMAL RECORDS

Teachers and students performing educational research will need to keep more formal records of each student's progress. If care has been taken to date each card as it is added to the word bank, the information will always be readily at hand and can be entered into the formal record file later.

We have already suggested a rough guide for ascertaining whether a child is ready for the symbol accentuation (SAW) approach. For the sake of teachers and researchers, we are now going to describe a more standardized procedure.

The Picture Vocabulary Test

The Picture Vocabulary Test provides a handy way of testing a pupil's receptive vocabulary by means of picture identification. Not only does this give one a guide to the pupil's vocabulary age, but it is also a test of a pupil's ability to recognize simple black and white drawings. This ability is a prerequisite to the symbol accentuation approach. Either Test 1 or the pre-school version can be used, depending upon the pupil's ability. The raw scores can be converted to a vocabulary age. Insufficient evidence is available to lay down the minimum vocabulary age required before a pupil can learn by the symbol accentuation method. Our research suggests that it is not appropriate to start until a pupil has a vocabulary age of three-and-a-half to four years.

Establishing a Baseline

Having ascertained a student's readiness to begin, the next thing is to discover whether he recognizes any printed words at all. It is not safe to assume that a student has no word recognition because he has not responded to flash cards. One of our teenage students had apparently a very limited ability—he recognized a few key words to literacy only. Yet he was later found to be able to recognize all the names of the NFL teams with no difficulty. When presented with these he remarked, "That's easy, it's The Atlanta Falcons." So in establishing a baseline, a student's own interests should be taken into consideration. One of the first words a student often recognizes is his own name and then, perhaps, the names of his friends. The size of print also seems crucial with some handicapped pupils.

With these considerations in mind, we prepared a series of cards printed in large letters (using a stencil, each short letter 0.3 inches high). The words we chose were the student's first name, the first names of his classmates, and a few very frequently occurring words, such as *Mommy*, *Daddy*, *bus*, *dog*, *cat*, *stop*, *go*, *school*, and *house*. Students are informally tested on these words. They are first tested for word recognition. Three words are placed on the desk, and the students are asked to pick out the one that says *Mary* or *John* (their own name). It is important not to drag out this procedure as it will have a negative effect on your student. If he fails on his own name and on five common words, then it should be discontinued. A few words pertaining to the student's special interest can then be tried. However, if the student is able to pick out any of the words from the display, he should be presented with these and asked to read them: "Do you know what that says?"

Page 139 shows a simple record of this baseline data.

Key Words to Literacy

If a student recognizes the names of his classmates and most of the additional familiar words, then he can be further tested using the Dolch Word Vocabulary list. These, also, should be printed on separate cards in large print as shown.

a and he I in is it

As before, he should first be tested for recognition and then for recall. As before, a record sheet should be filled in for each student.

NAME:_____ DATE OF BIRTH:_____

DATE OF TESTING:_____

NAMES OF CLASSMATES AND FAMILIAR WORDS

1.	☐	1. Mother	☐
2.	☐	2. Daddy	☐
3.	☐	3. bus	☐
4.	☐	4. dog	☐
5.	☐	5. cat	☐
6.	☐	6. stop	☐
7.	☐	7. go	☐
8.	☐	8. school	☐
9.	☐	9. house	☐

The procedure should be discontinued when the student fails on five consecutive words. Words that have been reliably recognized and recalled should be filed in the word bank and dated, and the letter *B* for baseline noted on the card. A pupil who is able to read twenty or more key words may be ready for a mixed approach to reading. New words can be introduced by means of symbol accentuation (see Chapter 1), but reading fluency can be facilitated by means of the language-experience

RECORDING PROGRESS

RECORD OF ACQUISITION OF SIGHT VOCABULARY BY SYMBOL ACCENTUATION

NAME: ..Mary..Smith........... DOB: ..1.1.63... CA: ...16..... MA: .5years...

AETIOLOGY: .Downs..Syndrome.................

SCHOOL: ....

STATUS OF TEACHER: TRAINED TEACHER, CLASSROOM ASSISTANT, PARENT, OTHER Parent..

BASELINE SIGHT VOCABULARY (enter actual words): .NONE............................

APPROXIMATE DURATION OF EACH SESSION: ....30..minutes.........

SESSION NUMBER	1	2	3	4	5	6	7														
DATES OF SESSIONS	3/3	10/3	17/3	21/3	28/3	4/4	11/4														
Mary	Ø	/	/	✓	⊗	✗	✗														
cat		Ø	/	✓	✓	⊗	✗														
cup			Ø	Ø	/	/	✓														
bed					Ø	/	✓														
gun						Ø	Ø														

KEY

O No recall (ie. cannot name it) of SA word
Ø Recall (ie. can name) SA word with prompts (ie. it mews etc.)
/ Recall of SA word without prompts on 3 spaced trials
✓ Recall and recognition of SA words (ie. can pick it out from 3 distractors)
   (no prompts) on 3 spaced trials
⊗ Recall of TO word with prompts
✗ Recall of TO word without prompts
✗ Recall and recognition of TO words

approach (see Chapter 3). This approach can be oriented to the child's own interest words, such as New York Jets.

Detailed Records of Progress Using Symbol Accentuation

Teachers using symbol-accentuation methods for the first time who are wishing to test its efficacy or researchers who wish to compare this method with other methods of acquiring a sight vocabulary will find the record sheet on the facing page simple to use, yielding a great deal of detailed information. The example has been partly filled in to indicate its use.

Simpler records can later be kept of words that qualify for the word bank.

CONCLUSION

This book is in many ways experimental. We do not really know how far we can go in stimulating handicapped students. Not all students will go all the way on these paths to literacy.

If your child has not gotten as far as reading independently, do not regard him as a failure. He will have learned some words—words that occur in the environment. He will have "learned to learn," he will very likely have increased his experience of the spoken language, and he will have had a lot of fun and stimulation. He may also have acquired some social skills and some independent behavior during his participation in games and reading activities.

Bibliography

The bibliography and recommended books and materials were compiled by the American editor, Sally B. Carter, because those selected by the authors were not available in the United States.

READINESS MATERIALS

The following is a list of books suitable for reading aloud. (See Chapter 6.)

For the Teacher

Anderson, Paul S. 1963. *Storytelling with the flannel board.* Minneapolis, Minn.: T. S. Denison.

Bailey, Carolyn S.; and Lewis, Clara M. 1965. *Favorite stories for the children's hour.* New York: Platt.

Corcoran, Gertrude. 1976. *Language experience for nursery and kindergarten years.* Itasca, Ill.: F. E. Peacock.

Gambell, Trevor J. 1976. *Developing children's language through the elementary school media centre.* ED 137 792. New York State Department of Education.

Henry, Mable Wright. 1967. *Creative experiences in oral language.* Urbana, Ill.: National Council of Teachers of English.

Huck, Charlotte S. 1976. *Children's literature in the elementary school.* 3rd ed. New York: Holt, Rinehart and Winston.

Listening and speaking, K-3: a packet for teachers. 1975. New York State Department of Education.

McIntyre, Barbara. 1974. *Creative drama in the elementary school.* Itasca, Ill.: F. E. Peacock.

Moffett, James. 1973. *A student center of language arts curriculum, grades K-6: a handbook for teachers.* Boston: Houghton Mifflin.

Possein, Wilma M. 1969. *They all need to talk.* New York: Appleton-Century-Crofts.

Russell, David; and Russell, Elizabeth. 1959. *Listening aids through the grades.* New York: Teachers College Press.

Spache, George D.; and Spache, Evelyn B. 1973. *Reading in the elementary school.* 3rd ed. Boston: Allyn and Bacon. (See pp. 119-123 and 128-129 for suggested materials to develop perceptual skills.)

Tooze, Ruth. 1959. *Storytelling.* New York: Prentice-Hall.

For Use with the Elementary School Student

Alpha time. Jackson, Miss.: Central School Supply.

A pocket guide of movement and activities for the elementary school by Marjorie Latchaw. Englewood Cliffs, N.J.: Prentice-Hall.

Creating with materials for work and play. Washington, D.C.: Association for Childhood Education International.

Developing prereading skills by Rachel G. Brake. New York: Holt, Rinehart and Winston.

Directionality program. Glendale, Calif.: Bowmar Records.

Kindergarten fun by Cole and Appleyard. Cincinnati, Ohio: McCormick-Mathers.

Kindergarten readiness. New York: Harper and Row.

Learning readiness system by Scott, Ratekin, Kramer, Nelson, and Dunbar. New York: Harper and Row.

Letters in words by Helen A. Murphy and Donald D. Durrell. Wellesley, Mass.: Curriculum Associates.

Listening-doing-learning tapes (Levels K-1) by Don Parker, Shelby Parker, and William Fryback. Chicago: Science Research Associates.

Listening time (Albums 1-3) by Louise Bender Scott, Glendale, Calif.: Bowmar Records, Inc.

Peabody early experience kit (Levels P-3) by Lloyd M. Dunn. Circle Pines, Minn.: American Guidance Service.

Peabody language kits (Levels P, I, II, III) by Lloyd M. Dunn et al. Circle Pines, Minn.: American Guidance Service.

Readiness for learning clinic by McLeod. Philadelphia: J. B. Lippincott.

SIGHT VOCABULARY MATERIALS

ABC Game. Buffalo, N.Y.: Kenworthy Educational Services.

Basic Sight Vocabulary Cards. Champaign, Ill.: Garrard.

Basic Word Concepts and Vocabulary Development Charts. Chicago: ETA Division of A. Daigger.

Build-It (Grades 3-8). Washington, D.C.: Remedial Education Press.

Dolch Games by E. W. Dolch. Includes *Basic Sight Word Cards*, *Group Word Teaching Game*, *Phrase Cards*, *Picture Word Cards*, *Popper Words*, *Who Gets It*. Champaign, Ill.: Garrard.

Educational Password Game. Springfield, Mass.: Milton Bradley.

Flash X, A Hand Tachistoscope for Rapid Word Recognition. Huntington, N.Y.: Educational Development Laboratories.

Match. Champaign, Ill.: Garrard.

Pictocabulary Series. Rockville Centre, N.Y.: Barnell Loft.

Picture Words for Beginners. Springfield, Mass.: Milton Bradley.

Rolling Reader. Glenview, Ill.: Scott, Foresman.

Spello Word Game, Oak Lawn, Ill.: Ideal.

The following is a list of books, compiled by the authors, with simple text that, when read aloud, can be readily understood by children. Aimed at the student with young interests.

TITLE	AUTHOR	PUBLISHER
The House that Jack Built	Galdone	Bodley Head
Old Mother Hubbard and her Dog	Galdone	Bodley Head
Story of 3 Bears	Stubbs	Bodley Head
Golden Goose	Stubbs	Bodley Head
Brer Rabbit Stories	Browne	BBC (Jackanory)
Seven Tales from H. C. Anderson	Le Gallienne	World's Word
London Bridge is Falling Down	Spier	World's Word
Reading with Winnie-the-Pooh (6 Booklets)	Garland	Nelson
More Fairy Stories from Grimm	William Ellis	Blackie
Cowboy Sam Series (9 Books)	Chandler	Arnold

The following are books, compiled by the authors, with a good storyline but needing adaptation or modification when read aloud.

TITLE	AUTHOR	PUBLISHER
Borrowers	Norton	American Pub.
Wombles Books	Beresford	"
Paddington Bear	Bond	"
Winnie-the-Pooh	Milne	"
Where the Wild Things Are	Sendak	"
The Hobbit	Tolkien	"
Beatrix Potter		"

HIGH-INTEREST-LOW VOCABULARY BOOKS

The following list of books and series can supplement a reading program by providing stories based on content above their readability level. Information on additional books is available from most of these publishers.

Alley Alligator Series, Benefic Press, Westchester, Ill. 60153. Stories center around three rangers and a baby alligator. Appropriate series for primary youngsters.

Breakthrough Series, Allyn & Bacon, 470 Atlantic Ave., Boston, Mass. 02210. Covers reading levels 2-6, with interest level appropriate for junior and senior high school. Well-written stories.

Checkered Flag Series, Field Education Publications, 2400 Hanover St., Palo Alto, Calif., 94002. Exciting stories appropriate for high school students and written on grade levels 2-5.

Deep-Sea Adventure Series, Harr Wagner Publishing, 609 Mission St., San Francisco, Calif. High interest, low vocabulary series with a controlled vocabulary and the same characters throughout the series. Grade level 2.5 through 6.

The Monster Books, Bowmar, Glendale, Calif. 91201. Series of beginning reading books using natural language patterns of young children. Pictures and stories are appealing to primary and intermediate age youngsters.

Mystery Adventure Series, Benefic Press, Westchester, Ill. 60153. Mystery stories involving a teen age boy and girl, appropriate for grades five through twelve with reading levels second through sixth.

Pacemaker Series, Fearon Publishing, 6 Davis Dr., Belmont, Calif. 94002. Appropriate for high school students reading on grade levels 2-3.

Pal Paperbacks, Xerox Education Publications, Columbus, Ohio 43216. Highly entertaining and exciting stories in paperback format. The stories are truly high interest, low vocabulary. Appropriate for middle school and higher.

Play the Game, Bowmar, Glendale, Calif. 91201. A high interest, low vocabulary series appropriate for high school level. Controlled vocabulary stories feature the lives of famous athletes.

Reader's Digest Skill Builders, Reader's Digest Services, Inc., Educational Division, Pleasantville, N.Y. 10570. Short interesting stories followed by activities on word attack and comprehension skills. Available on all levels, 1st grade to books appropriate for adult level remediation.

Reading Incentive Program, Bowmar, Glendale, Calif. 91201. Twenty high interest subjects are combined into a very motivating program for intermediate thru high school age students. Each title has a book, a filmstrip, and skill development sheets that are excellent. Some of the subjects covered include motorcycles, horses, surfing, dogs, and hot air balloons.

Sports Mystery Series, Benefic Press, Westchester, Ill. 60153. Fast paced adventure stories for children grades fourth through twelfth, with reading levels second through fourth grade.

The following are some introductory reading programs with a phonic approach. (See Chapter 7.)

Basic Primary Phonics (filmstrips). Chicago: Society for Visual Eucation.

Discovering Phonics We Use. Chicago: Rand McNally and Company.

The Ginn Word Enrichment Program by Theodore Clymer et al. Boston: Ginn and Company.

Merrill Phonics Skilltexts and Skilltapes by Josephine B. Wolfe. Columbus, Ohio: Charles E. Merrill.

New Phonics Skilltexts. Columbus, Ohio: Charles E. Merrill.

The New Phonics We Use Learning Kits. Chicago: Rand McNally and Company.

Open Court Basic Readers by Arthur S. Trace, ed. La Salle, Ill.: Open Court Publishing Company.

Phonetic Analysis by Virginia Middlemas et al. New York: Center for Programmed Instruction.

Phonetic Keys to Reading and *Keys to Independence in Reading* by Theodore M. Harris et al. Oklahoma City: The Economy Company.

Phonics and Word Power. Columbus, Ohio: Ameican Education Publications.

Phonics Plus by Charles T. Mangrum II and Peter B. Messmore. Englewood Cliffs, N.J.: Prentice-Hall.

Phonics Practice (filmstrips). Chicago: Science Research Associates.

Reading with Phonics by E. C. Wingo and Mary C. Hletko. Phildelphia: J. B. Lippincott Company.

Speech-to-Print Phonics: A Phonics Foundation for Reading by Donald A. Durrell and Helen A. Murphy. New York: Harcourt Brace Jovanovich.

SRA Reading Laboratory I-World Games (grades 1-6). Chicago: Science Research Associates.

SRA Skills Series. Chicago: Science Research Associates.

Steck Teaching Aids. Austin, Texas: The Steck Company.

Take and Vowel Lotto by E. W. Dolch. Champaign, Ill.: Garrard Publishing Company.

Word Analysis Charts by William Kottmeyer and Kay Ware. St. Louis: Webster Publishing Company.

Word Rummy. Detroit: Educational Cards.

REFERENCES AND SUGGESTIONS FOR FURTHER READING

Aukerman, R.C. *Approaches to beginning reading.* New York: John Wiley & Sons, 1971. A good source book that reviews the major initial reading approaches, discussing philosophy, development, and research.

Duffy, G.G., & Sherman, G.B. *Systematic reading instruction.* New York: Harper & Row, 1972. A highly structured approach to reading. The sequencing is extremely involved but excellent for seriously disabled readers.

Bond, G.L., & Tinker, M.A. *Reading difficulties: Their diagnosis and correction.* New York: Appleton-Century-Crofts, 1957. Good survey of the causes, diagnoses, and remediation of reading problems.

Buckley, L.A., & Cullvin, A. *Picnic of sounds: A playful approach to reading.* New York: Citation Press, 1975. A resource book for teaching a beginning sound program. It includes approaches, word lists, and activities.

Farnette, C., Forte, I., & Loss, B. *Kid's stuff: Reading and writing readiness.* Nashville, Tenn.: Incentive Publications, Inc., 1969. Book of teaching strategies, simple management system, teacher resources, activities and student pages ready to reproduce. Suitable for teaching on the primary and intermediate level.

Goodman, K.S. (Ed.) *Miscue analysis.* Urbana, Illinois: ERIC Clearinghouse on Reading and Communication Skills, 1973. Edited volume that presents several informative chapters on the use of miscue analysis in diagnosis.

Gillespie, P.H., & Johnson, L. *Teaching reading to the mildly retarded child.* Columbus, Ohio: Charles E. Merrill Publishing Co., 1974. Excellent text on reading characteristics of the retarded, detailed assessment procedures and remedial approaches.

Gillham, W.E.C. *Teaching a child to read.* London: Hodder and Stoughton, 1976.

Gunzburg, H.C. *Social competence and social handicap.* London: Bailliere, Tindall and Cassell, 1968.

Heilman, A.W. *Phonics in proper perspective.* Columbus, Ohio: Charles E. Merrill Publishing Co., 1968. An excellent handbook on the mechanics and sequential progression of phonics.

Jeffree, D.M. and Cheseldine, S. *Pathways to independence.* Seven Oaks, Hodder and Stoughton, 1982.

Jeffree D.M. and McConkey, R. Let me speak. London: Souvenir Press, 1976.

Jeffree, D.M. McConkey, R. and Hewson, S. *Let me play.* London, Souvenir Press, 1977.

Matthes, C. *How children are taught to read.* Lincoln, Nebraska: Professional Educators Publications, 1972. Gives brief descriptions, strengths, weaknesses, and research on the most commonly used reading approaches.

Miller, A. and Miller, E.E. "Symbol accentuation: the perceptual transfer of meaning from spoken to printed words." *American Journal of Mental Deficiency.* 76 (1968) 110-17.

Orton, J.L. *A guide to teaching phonics.* Cambridge, Mass.: Educators Publishing Service. 1964, 1975. Handbook on the Orton approach to phonics. Sequential lessons with complete word lists and activities.

Otto, W., McMenemy, R.A., & Smith, R.J. *Corrective and remedial teaching.* Boston: Houghton-Mifflin, 1973. An all encompassing book covering the diagnosis and remediation of all academic areas. Highly recommended for all teachers of special children.

Russell, D.H., & Karp, E.E. *Reading aids through the grades.* New York: Columbia University Teachers College, 1961.

Provides over 300 activities to be used for readiness to junior high school reading levels.

Spache, E.B. *Reading activities for child involvement.* Boston. Allyn & Bacon, Inc., 1976. Collection of 472 activities covering all areas of reading. The book's organization and cross referencing of activities by skill areas adds to its usability.

Stauffer, R.S. *The language experience approach to the teaching of reading.* New York: Harper & Row, 1970. Provides theoretical foundations and practical assistance for teachers interested in using the LEA approach. Includes discussion of LEA's usage in special education classes.

Wallen, C.J. *Competency in teaching reading.* Chicago: Science Research Associates, 1972. A book designed to aid teachers in developing diagnostic reading-teaching abilities It is a self-contained, in-depth, reading program for training teachers.

Index